GENEALOGY FOR BEGINNERS

Genealogy
for Beginners

Arthur J. Willis
F.R.I.C.S., F.S.G.
and
Molly Tatchell
B.A.

PHILLIMORE

1984

First published 1955
by Ernest Benn Limited

Second Edition revised, 1970

Third Edition revised, 1976

Fourth Edition revised, 1979

Fifth Edition revised, 1984

Reprinted, 1987

by Phillimore & Co. Ltd.,
Shopwyke Hall, Chichester, Sussex, England

ISBN 0 85033 346 6

Printed and bound in Great Britain by
BILLINGS BOOK PLAN
Worcester, England

CONTENTS

LIST OF PLATES

CHART

ABBREVIATIONS USED

P.P.R.	Principal Probate Registry (Somerset House)
P.C.C.	Prerogative Court of Canterbury
P.C.Y.	Prerogative Court of York
P.R.O.	Public Record Office
B.L.	The British Library
Add. MSS.	Additional Manuscripts in the British Library

Note

Names and areas of counties are as existing before the 1974 reorganisation

I cannot but condemn the carelessness, not to say ingratitude, of those . . . who can give no better account of the place where their fathers and grand-fathers were born, than the child unborn . . . I could almost wish that a moderate fine were imposed on such heirs, whose fathers were born before them, and yet they know not where they were born.

Thomas Fuller: *The Worthies of England* 1662

ACKNOWLEDGEMENTS

OUR THANKS are due to those who have given permission for the reproduction of photocopies. The source is acknowledged at the foot of each plate.

We are indebted to Mrs. J. Cox and Mrs. S. Lumas of the Public Record Office, Mr. A. Camp, Director of the Society of Genealogists, and Mrs. K. E. Proudfoot for help and suggestions.

A.J.W.
M.T.

PREFACE

A STRIKING result of the ever-increasing interest in genealogy in recent years has been the publication of large numbers of books and pamphlets dealing with various aspects of the subject. Among the latter are the leaflets issued by the Public Record Office, the Society of Genealogists, the Federation of Family History Societies and the British Library. For this reason, and because some of the earlier works have been superseded or are long out of print, a completely revised bibliography has been provided for this edition, together with references in the text to recent publications where appropriate.

Among changes that have taken place since the last edition have been the release of the 1881 Census Returns, the transfer of indexes of death certificates to Alexandra House, and, of course, the inevitable rise in the cost of all certificates, making early recourse to the Census Returns even more desirable. A note has been made of the improved aids now provided in the Census Room still, happily, in Portugal Street, and of the excellent reference guide on the subject provided by the Public Record Office—one among a number of guides specially aimed at the genealogist.

The importance of the International Genealogical Index (formerly known as the Computer File Index or 'Mormon Microfiche') is emphasised by its now being available in a number of local record offices. Its usefulness is still further increased when, as at the Society of Genealogists, a reader-printer is available for making copies.

In this new edition improvement has been made in the quality of the plates so that these may be more easily studied with reference to the text.

We should emphasise that we are dealing with England and Wales only. Conditions are different in Scotland, and Ireland has special difficulties owing to loss of records.

A.J.W.
M.T.

Since writing the above the sad news has been received of the death of Mr. Arthur J. Willis. This present work and his other important contributions to genealogical research will remain as a lasting memorial to him.

1984   M.T.

PREFACE TO THE FIRST EDITION

AN INTEREST in genealogy need not be limited to those who are hoping to trace their descent from the Norman invaders, to revive a dormant peerage or, perhaps, just to gate-crash into 'County' society. There is much in the subject of interest for the ordinary man. We knew our fathers and probably our grandfathers. We may have heard tell of a great-grandfather. Who was he? What did he do? There is often little direct knowledge handed down, but, even if he had no exalted position, there is fairly certainly information about him somewhere—parish records, wills, local newspapers and similar sources. The records of his town or county may have lists of inhabitants, and these sometimes contain information as to place of business or residence. If he was a Town Councillor or interested in some local projects, charitable or otherwise, he may appear in the local archives. He may even be found in the records of the relief of the poor, or, perhaps, of the Quarter Sessions! A number of small details can be collected which together may give some sort of picture.

Then what about his father? Information is naturally more difficult to find as one goes back, but, even if there is little detail about earlier generations, it may be quite possible, given a little luck, to trace the pedigree back to the 17th or even 16th century from parish registers, wills and other sources.

In making research into my own family pedigree I felt the need of an elementary guide on how to set about the undertaking, what to look for and where, the ordinary difficulties likely to be encountered and how they might be overcome. I was doing the research in spare time, so anything which would save me time in investigating

methods of approach would be valuable. I could find
nothing in the way of textbooks, except two or three
small handbooks, which by trying to embrace too much
gave little information of value to me. I have found in
another sphere how much a textbook is appreciated on
the very elements of a subject, untrammelled by the
complications of more advanced work, and I thought that
an elementary book, answering the queries and difficulties
that I myself had met in my genealogical expedition,
might be of value to others first taking up the subject,
whether as a hobby or as a profession. I have, in Part I of
the book, tried to meet this need.

May I emphasise that this is a book for beginners. The
writing is focussed on them and their needs: the expert
cannot expect to find much, if anything, new. I am
limiting myself to what might give the novice a start,
and am excluding any consideration of the very early
times (when both parish registers and regular records of
wills are rare or non-existent) and of the remoter
possibilities in later times. By the time any investigator
has reached, say, the middle of the 16th century or has
examined all the more normal sources of evidence in the
later period he is more than a novice.

The plates are necessarily reduced in printing, but will
be found to read clearly with the magnifying glass which
should be in every genealogist's pocket.

In Part II I have given an account of the researches into
my own family pedigree, and the relative tables necessary
to follow it will be found on the chart*. This account is but
an example, an illustration of how a search can work out.
If one is set a problem in geometry one does not expect
to find all the standard theorems applied; some only will

*Pages 190-196.

be needed. In the same way, this account does not hope to incorporate all the possible lines of research. It describes those which in a particular case were followed, some with success, some without. Some, such as the examination of parish registers, wills, etc., are essential to almost any search, some may or may not be suitable in other cases and one or two arose from the particular circumstances of the particular family and may never be applicable elsewhere. In other circumstances, moreover, there will be other methods of approach not touched on in the example. I hope that the account will convey something of the atmosphere of a search as well as provide suggestions as to methods and procedure. In preparing for an examination in geometry one will work out problems in past examination papers, not because the same will be set again, but because the course of reasoning may be useful in answering other questions.

I feel, too, that a real live example should be of value in showing that research need not be a dry-as-dust affair, but can be combined with light (and sometimes comic) relief in unveiling the lives of the individuals. I look on genealogy as something more than merely obtaining proof of descent: it is to me an attempt to answer the question 'Can these bones live?'

1955   A.J.W.

Chapter One

HOW TO BEGIN

THE PREPARATION of a pedigree must always start at the latest known generation and work backwards. It will generally be unwise to start with someone of the same name in the Elizabethan era and try to follow his descendants through to the individual of the present day. The person who wants his pedigree traced will usually be the one from whom to build backwards. In the first instance he will probably want to trace his male line, but the scope for genealogical research is infinite, as search can later be made for the descent of his mother through her father, then of his two other grandparents, and so on almost *ad infinitum.*

First will come the personal knowledge of the individual concerned. He will know the names of father and mother, brothers and sisters, uncles and aunts and quite probably grandfather. These names can be set out spaced well apart in the form shown on the pedigree.*
In setting out brothers and sisters some genealogists put all the males first on the left-hand side (dexter to heralds) presumably because the females are unimportant for the purpose of following through the surname, but I prefer myself to keep the order of age, even if the lines of descent on the table must dance from side to side. It will be seen in the example that by thickening the lines the main descent can be made to stand out.

The older members of the family may have information from their own knowledge or recollection which can be

*Pedigree of the WILLIS family (pages 190-196).

invaluable. Opportunity should be taken to ask them to help by telling what they know, not merely of the line of descent but of the history of the family, work and character of individuals, etc. There may be traditions handed down from one generation to another, probably verbally. These should be recorded, but, of course, as tradition, not as definite knowledge. It is dangerous to accept tradition without some confirmation.

Speaking of traditions, one of the commonest of these is the connection with some armigerous family giving the right to bear arms. It may, of course, be true, but should be suspect until confirmed. In the 19th century, particularly, 'heraldic stationers' developed their publicity, and rings and notepaper with heraldic crests became common. Heraldry will not be touched on here, though it is, of course, of value in genealogical research on families known to be entitled to arms. There is no official roll of arms published, and those interested must depend on the various books which deal with the genealogy of the peerage and gentry. However, in all printed records one must remember that an entry in print is not *ipso facto* correct, putting a fact beyond question. There may be mistakes in copying, in interpretation or in typography, or the original itself may be suspect.

Whilst personal knowledge will establish relationships, this must be supplemented by such evidence as may be available from family documents as to dates of births, marriages and deaths. In the 18th and 19th centuries it was common for a family to have a large 'family bible'. On the fly leaves of this, or sometimes on blank pages between Old and New Testaments were written out details about members of that family. Dates and places of births, baptisms, marriages, deaths and burials were usually recorded and often other information, such as who the husbands or wives of members of the family were. A typical example of an extract from a family bible is given on Plate 3. If there is no family bible, there may be certificates of birth, baptism, etc., amongst family documents, from which the same information can be obtained. If there is reluctance to ask a particular aunt her age, it will not usually be difficult to lead her to talking sufficiently of her family to extract her maiden name (if married) and her place of birth: then a search at the General Register Office* (*see* page 14) should find the date of birth without difficulty, particularly if it is known approximately.

The next most valuable documents likely to be found in family archives are wills of earlier generations. A father usually (though not, of course, always) mentions his wife and all his children living at the time of its execution. If, for instance, the grandfather being known, a great grandfather's will is available his name can be added as well as those of the grandfather's brothers and sisters. If the copy should be the official probate copy, the date and place of probate should be added in the pedigree.

All old wills of members of the family should be examined, whether in the direct male line or not, as sometimes a gap in one will (perhaps a son who died before its execution) may be filled from another (e.g. from that of an aunt who died earlier, whilst the son was still alive). The wills of aunts and uncles are particularly useful, as often mentioning great-nephews and great-nieces.

Besides a family bible and old wills there will possibly be other family documents, the quantity of which will depend on the importance of the family and the care which has been taken to preserve them. It may be that some earlier member of the family has been interested and

*Now part of the Office of Population Censuses and Surveys (O.P.C.S.).

has left some notes. All should be examined for any information bearing on the pedigree.

There may be no family documents to provide this
foundation for the pedigree. A man may have lost his
parents at an early age and have been brought up by,
perhaps, two aunts. Such oral information as can be
gleaned from them should be noted first. They will probably be able to say something of the father and, perhaps,
of the grandfather (their own father). Information may be
vague on some points, but an effort should be made to
have it as definitely as possible, particularly dates of
births, marriages and deaths* and the places where they
occurred.

When confirmation of such records is required, a visit
should be paid to the General Register Office at St.
Catherine's House, Kingsway, London, W.C.2, where
indexes can be seen for all births, marriages and deaths
in England and Wales since 1 July, 1837.† From that date
civil registration began, returns being sent to the General
Register Office by District Registrars and, in the case of
marriages in Church, by the incumbent of the parish.
Indexes may be searched without charge: they normally
give surname, Christian name and registration district
only, so the searcher should be armed with approximate
dates and places. The original registers are not open for
public inspection, but, when the required entry has been
found in the index, a form will be completed and a full
certificate of the birth, marriage or death will be supplied
for a fee of £5 on personal search. This certificate
can either be sent by post or collected some days later.
The information given by certificates is:

---

*Indexes to death certificates are now at Alexandra House,
Kingsway. Certificates are still applied for in the main building.

†6 and 7 Will. IV, c.85 and 86.

Births: date and place of birth, full names, names of parents, occupation of father and particulars of the informant.

Marriages: date of marriage, full names and ages of the parties, whether bachelor, spinster or widowed, occupations and addresses, full names and occupations of fathers of each party, place and form of marriage and names of witnesses.

Deaths: date and place of death, full name, sex, age, profession, cause of death and particulars of the informant.

Certificates of birth, marriage or death can be applied for by letter: the search fee for a period of five years is in this case £10,* including the certificate. It is important that the precise details known should be given, i.e., surname and Christian name with date and place of the event (as nearly as is known). Such application can also be made to the local District Registrar.

A word of warning—if the place of birth was a small village, this will not be given as the registration district in the index: this would probably be the name of the nearest town, or the Hundred. It is therefore advisable to familiarise oneself with the area by studying the map before going to St. Catherine's House.

The General Register Office includes not only records of England and Wales, but also those of registration with British Consulates abroad, at which it is customary for British subjects to register births, marriages and deaths. One must not, therefore, necessarily be disheartened because an ancestor is found to have gone abroad.

If there is some doubt whether the certificate applied for is the right one, e.g. if two persons of the same name occur in the same registration district in the same period,

*Fees quoted as at 1 April 1984.

one can ask for a check to be made (at an additional charge).

In view of the high charges for certificates, the searcher will want to cut down on them as much as possible. With this in mind he could make a search in the census returns described in the next chapter for 1851, 1861, 1871 or 1881, whichever is nearest to the date.

For example, suppose that a birth has been found for 1863. A search of the Census for 1861 would be well worth while. If the family is found, the place of birth of each member would be given and, with luck, a grand-parent might be found living in the same household. This might take one back in one step to the period before civil registration and directly to the parish registers without need for further certificates. If, however, the family is not found in the parish of the 1863 birth, one should try the 1871 census. It is worth while remembering that the entry of a brother or sister is equally valuable.

Chapter Two

CENSUS RETURNS

A CENSUS has been taken in England and Wales every ten years from 1801 (except in 1941 during the War). The earlier ones, which did not give names, have not, with one exception, survived, and those less than 100 years old are not yet open to inspection. But the Census Returns for 1841, 1851, 1861, 1871 and 1881 can be seen at the Public Record Office Census Room in Portugal Street on microfilm.

Of the above censuses, that for 1841 is the least useful. It gives the names, ages (within five years) and occupations of all persons in the household, but it does not give place of birth, beyond stating whether or not the individual was born in the county of residence.

The returns for 1851, 1861, 1871 and 1881 are more useful, for not only do they give the exact age (as alleged) and the relationship of the members of the household to one another, but, most important of all, they give the place of birth. In the case of a village or small town, it should then be easy to pin-point the parish register. Sometimes in the case of a large town or city, the parish of birth is given. If not, it can mean a search of a number of registers (not forgetting the non-parochial ones). If place of birth is simply given as 'London', then one's heart truly sinks, as it can be a case of looking for the proverbial needle in a haystack.

No charge is made for inspection of Census Returns, and a day pass may be obtained at the door of the office in Portugal Street. The Census Room is open

Monday to Friday 9.30 to 4.50 p.m. except the usual public holidays, and a two weeks closure in October, concerning which enquiry should be made. Notices on the walls of the search room explain means of reference, and the attendants are always willing to help those in difficulties, but a few comments might here prove useful.

There are two sets of volumes for each census, and from these one can obtain the reference number for the parish required. In 1841 the parishes are arranged by hundred or wapentake; in the other censuses they are arranged by registrar's enumeration district. Once the parish has been located in the hundred or district, the hand-written numbers in the margin show the correct bundle number. This should be entered on the application form, preceded by the appropriate prefix: 1841 and 1851 HO 107; 1861 RG 9; 1871 RG 10; 1881 RG 11.

For London and large towns and cities exact addresses are essential in order to avoid an endless search. London directories for 1841 to 1881 are available in the search room; some others may be asked for at the desk (a list can be consulted).

There is a list showing availability of street indexes for various towns, and also for some country areas, e.g., Cornwall. The indexes are in volumes to be found with the other lists and indexes for each census.

If no street index is available, as is often the case with small country towns, one can, when examining the actual census returns, refer to the list of streets etc. which prefaces each sub-district.

Many libraries and local record offices now hold microfilm copies of census returns which relate to their own area, and it is worth making enquiries about these before going to the Census Room in Portugal Street.*

*See also J. S. W. Gibson, *Census Returns on Microfilm, a Directory to Local Holdings* (3rd edn., 1981).

It is possible in certain circumstances to obtain information from census records for 1891 and 1901 for a search fee of £14.75. Only age and place of birth of named persons at an address precisely given will be supplied, but only on behalf of direct descendants. Application should be made at St. Catherine's House.

A quick copying photographic service is available in the Census Room, and photocopies may be obtained by post providing that the full correct reference is given (*see* P.R.O. Reference Guide No. 19).

For general instructions on searching the Census, see P.R.O. Reference Guide No. 18.

Chapter Three

RECORDS OF SEARCHES

ONE OF THE DIFFICULTIES in searching is to know how to find what one wants. Much depends on the availability of lists and indexes. Much wanted information may be available somewhere, but cannot be found because there is no guide. The searcher should, therefore, discover if there is any guide to the information he wants. This may be in one of several forms.

List: A series of titles only, usually arranged alphababetically or by dates. They serve as a general classification of the records—an index to indexes. Such are the Class Lists at the P.R.O.

Index: an alphabetically arranged list of some particular aspect of the records, e.g., of subjects, places or names. Sometimes these are combined into a general index. For the genealogist, to whom names are usually the most important, indexes, if reliable, can save much time which might be wasted on vain searches.

Inventory: a list prepared in the order of finding or receipt, such as the printed Catalogues to the Additional MSS. at the B.L., in which the acquisitions are entered in order of the serial numbers given them on receipt. In that particular case the inventories, being amplified by a short account of each document and an alphabetical index, are given the more ambitious name of catalogue (*see* below).

Calendar: a list arranged by dates rather than alphabetically, though there may be alphabetical arrangement within the same date or group of dates, as in a calendar of wills. Often a short *précis* of each item is given, as in the *Calendars of State Papers.*

Catalogue: any enumeration arranged in an orderly and systematic way for assistance in searching. It is a more generic and full-dress term than those preceding.

It is essential that a careful record should be kept of all searches made and that such records should be available in a classified form, so that any particular item can be easily turned up. For taking records an A4 notebook could be used, or loose sheets of A4 paper. The first taking down will fairly certainly be in pencil (in some cases the use of ink is not allowed by the authority in charge of the documents for fear of marking and damage). Each record made should be marked with its source and reference, e.g., B.L. Add. MSS. 6211, fol. 199, so that it can easily be verified at any time.

Some may be deterred from undertaking genealogical research because they know that Latin was commonly used until comparatively recent times and because their knowledge of the language is scanty. Though some Latin may be met with, it is only before the middle of the 18th century that the language is really prevalent. Even then much of the Latin used, e.g., in the probate of wills, was of a stereotyped form: the meaning of this once understood can easily be applied to other cases, and all the reader will require is the ability to pick out the date, and, perhaps, distinguish between the root episcop- (bishop) and archidiacon- (archdeacon). There may, of course, be cases, e.g., legal records, which were in Latin until the Act of 1731,* where translation will be required, and this must be referred to an expert. A knowledge of classical Latin will need some adaptation to read the dog-Latin legal language, and reference may be necessary to such a book as *Revised Medieval Latin Word List* (Oxford U.P.) or *The Record Interpreter* (Phillimore). The former, though mainly

*4 Geo. II, c. 26.

for medieval words, includes many ecclesiastical or legal technical terms which continue as long as Latin was used and will not be found in a dictionary of classical Latin. The latter book, besides having a glossary of Latin words on a smaller scale than the former, gives very good lists of latinised Christian names, surnames, place names and abbreviations, which may without such a book of reference be puzzling. The list of the latinised forms of the names of bishoprics is particularly useful, if one is confronted with, say, the see of some strange Irish bishop.

It will be found useful as soon as possible after making the record to copy it in ink (or type) on to sheets of, say, A4 paper, each variety of entry being on a separate sheet, so that their order can be rearranged. These sheets can then be kept permanently in some sort of loose leaf binding, either perforated for the fastening or in a spring-back cover. As they accumulate it will be necessary to divide them into several volumes, keeping some sort of classification, e.g., one volume for parish register records, another for wills, etc. A sundry volume can be sub-divided by index tabs with such sections as MSS., newspapers, title deeds, and others which will suggest themselves in each case. If reference is wanted to any particular item, recollection of the form it took will enable it to be found quickly. If two separate lines are being traced, e.g., a father's and a mother's ancestry, it will be found advisable to keep the records entirely separate.

One should emphasise that it is just as important to keep a record of searches which produce no result as of those which do. I have more than once found myself looking at something which I had seen before, because I had not recorded that I had seen it. Much time can be wasted in that way.

It is worth while, too, recording all mentions of the family name, even if there is no evidence of relationship. Unexpected evidence may turn up later showing a connection and it may be very difficult to find the reference again.

It is well to make a practice of always recording dates by giving the day of the month first, then the month and the year, e.g., 2 December 1839 or even 1839 December 2, not December 2 1839. This prevents any confusion between the figures of day and year. Where months are abbreviated, e.g., Jan., Jun., Jul., writing must be quite clear or mistakes may be made.

Where entries have been found in parish registers before 1837, it may be thought advisable to obtain formal certificates from the incumbent, at any rate in the case of baptisms in the direct male line. A fee will be payable for these certificates (*see* page 29), and applications for them should state the name and date, whether baptism, marriage or burial and be sent with remittance and a stamped addressed envelope to the incumbent.

Other important evidence may be photographed, both as a convenience for reference and as a precaution against loss of the original. Though the latter is unlikely with documents in public custody, war has been the cause of many lost documents and, when in private custody particularly, there is always the risk of fire. Such authorities as the British Library, the Public Record Office or the Principal Probate Registry (and sometimes District Registries) will arrange for the provision of photo-prints, the cost of which is a good deal less than normal photography. Where the authority does not provide these facilities, they may be willing to send the document in their own charge to a local photo-printing firm, if there is one. If there is no such firm, the document will have to be photographed in the normal way; there is not usually any difficulty in obtaining permission for this to be done on the premises in which the document is kept, but a fee will be payable. Where documents are faint, in the case of photography, the expert will use what means he can to get the best reproduction. In the case of public authorities who themselves arrange for photo-copies, permission should be asked if the reproduction is to be published and this is usually readily given. Some authorities, however, will not allow certain photo-printing processes to be used on old documents, as they think that the documents might suffer damage.

Those interested in genealogy are normally in one of two categories: either the individual tracing his own family as a matter of personal interest and hobby, or somebody tracing ancestry for a specific purpose, such as connection with an armigerous family, a matter of inheritance or other legal reason. In the first case proof has to satisfy only the searcher's conscience (which may vary in strictness with individuals), but in the latter it must satisfy the investigation of experts and have a legal standing. If serious proof is likely to be demanded, the original evidence of each step (or a photoprint of it) should be kept with the pedigree so that it is there equally today or a hundred years hence.

Chapter Four

PARISH REGISTERS

UNTIL THE ORDER of Thomas Cromwell in 1538 there was no obligation to record baptisms, marriages and burials, though there are a few registers from an earlier date still extant. From that year the incumbent of the parish was required to keep such a record, but nevertheless a large number of the earliest registers have not survived. They were paper books at first until in 1597 it was ordered that they should be of parchment. Then they were apparently mostly transcribed, perhaps not without errors in so doing. Early volumes are in many cases missing, so one will face an advantage or handicap of good or bad luck in the search of a particular parish. It was also ordained in 1597 that copies of the register entries should be made and forwarded to the diocesan authorities. These copies are known as the 'Bishops' transcripts' and should be available to fill gaps where the original registers are lost, but, unfortunately, particularly in the earlier years, gaps will be found in these too.

During the Civil War, when what are known as Commonwealth 'intruders' took over parishes to the exclusion of the regular incumbents, the keeping of the registers became irregular. In 1653 under the Commonwealth the incumbent was often deprived of his authority over the registers, the keeping of which was transferred to a layman called a 'Register'. The solemnization of marriages was also soon after taken from the incumbent and the duty transferred to the justices. It will be found, therefore, that records of marriages during the Civil War and Commonwealth are

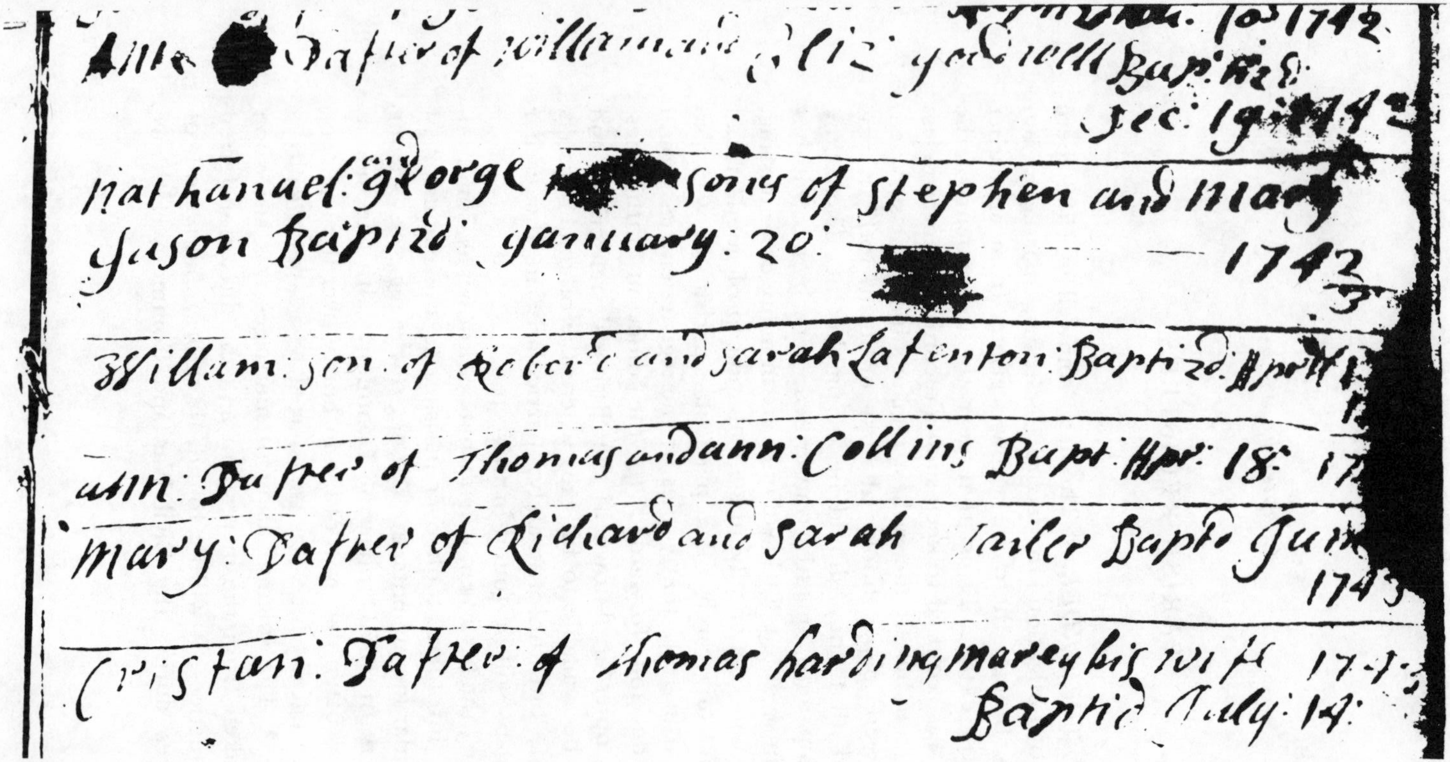
Anne Dafter of William and Eliz yardwell Baptized Jec: 19 1742
Nathanael and George sones of Stephen and Mary Jason Baptized January: 20 1742/3
William son of Robert and Sarah Latenton Baptized April
Ann Dafter of Thomas and Ann Collins Bapt Nov: 18 17
Mary Dafter of Richard and Sarah Tailer Bapt Jun 1743
Cristan Dafter of Thomas harding marey his wife 1743 Baptized July 14

Plate 1. Entries from a Parish Register (from the Parish Register (vol. 2) of Faccombe, Hants).
(*Reproduced by courtesy of the Hampshire Record Office*)

often either missing or incomplete, though fortunately the record of baptisms and burials may be found more regularly kept. The period and extent of the irregularity varies. In 1662 the intruders, if they did not 'conform', were often ejected.

In 1754, following Lord Hardwicke's Marriage Act,* record was to be kept of banns as well as marriages and the register was to be signed by the parties. Books of printed forms became available for this. They are not always to be found, but should be looked for.

Under Rose's Act of 1812† the registers were to be kept in three separate volumes in official printed form, and in smaller parishes where there are few entries the baptisms and burial volumes will be found still in use to this day.

On 1 July 1837 the system of civil registration now in force began, as has already been mentioned.‡ Baptism and burial (as distinct from birth and death) records were continued in the churches. Marriages, instead of being included in the bishop's transcripts were returned in the standard form to the Registrar General, though they are found to a limited extent in the transcript.

Copies exist in manuscript or printed form of a large number of the parish registers and these are most easily accessible to the public.** To search in a particular parish one should first look up to see whether such a copy is available, as much time and journeying can be saved by seeing a copy; moreover, it is much easier to read than the early handwriting of the original. The period covered by the copy should be noted, as some copies are for limited periods only, also whether all entries have been copied, as sometimes only the marriage

*26 Geo. II, c.33.   †52 Geo. III, c.146.   ‡Page 14.

**See *Parish Register Copies: part 1, the Society of Genealogists' Collection* (Society of Genealogists, 1970) and subsequent editions; *Parish Register Copies: part 2, other than the Society of Genealogists' Collection* (Society of Genealogists, 1971) and subsequent editions.

records are transcribed. These, however, may provide a possible outline of the pedigree required, to be confirmed and filled in by reference to baptisms and burials in the original registers. The practice, however (which still often prevails today), of the marriage taking place in the bride's parish means that the whole line of marriages will probably not be found in the same church. Fortunately, in earlier times before the development of transport there was little movement away from the neighbourhood and a missing marriage may quite likely be found in an adjoining parish, if the register is extant for the period.

Boyd's Marriage Index (*see* page 68) will be found useful, as, being alphabetical, it gives quick reference to a name so saving a search through a long copy of a register. It is not, of course, complete, particularly as many registers have been copied since its compilation.

If there is no copy of the required parish register or if the copy records marriages only, an opportunity will be taken to examine the originals and extract from them the baptisms and burials of the name and marriages if required. Even if marriages have been copied it sometimes happens that this examination will throw light on names which, in the old-time writing, were doubtful to the copyist. The name may be confirmed from baptism and burial entries which the copyist did not see. I have, too, in comparing a printed copy with the original found useful information omitted from the copy, such as the trade or parish of the person recorded or such a description as 'widow'.

If a marriage has not been found in a printed register, one should not despair, but refer to the originals, as copies are not by any means free from mistakes. The misreading of an initial in transcribing may put one quite off the scent.

The coming into force of the Parochial Registers and Records Measure (1978) on 1 January 1979 means that more and more parish registers are being deposited in local record offices and libraries. At the time of writing some 75% of registers have been deposited, and no doubt this proportion will rapidly increase.* The genealogist is therefore advised to consult the local record office or library before applying to the church for permission to search a particular register.

In view of the greatly increased number of people wishing to consult registers at record offices, it is advisable to telephone in advance to book a seat, and to order production of the registers required. In some cases (at the Greater London Record Office, for example) many registers are now on microfilm, and it is necessary to book a microfilm-reader some time in advance.

No search fees are payable when registers are deposited, except in the case of libraries which are not supported by the local authorities, e.g. the Borthwick Institute at York, the Bodleian Library in Oxford, and perhaps Cathedral Libraries.

In cases where the registers are still with the incumbent, an appointment should be made with him, and a stamped addressed envelope for reply should always be enclosed.

The fee for parish register searching at a church was fixed by the Parochial Fees Order in January 1982 at £3 for the first hour and £2 for every subsequent hour or part thereof. For longer searches some arrangement can usually be made with the incumbent, who will sometimes refuse to take a fee, but will welcome any contribution to the church funds.

If one has to refer to an incumbent, it must be realised that the attitude of the clergy to the registers varies. One man may feel very responsible and insist that examination

*For a guide to registers deposited, with the dates they cover, see *Original Parish Registers in Record Offices and Libraries*, Local Population Studies, 1974, and subsequent supplements; *National Index of Parish Registers* (Society of Genealogists, 1974-).

is made in his presence. On the other hand it has been
known for a vestry cupboard or chest to be found
unlocked and the registers accessible.

If there is no reply, even though a stamped addressed
envelope was enclosed, this may be due to the incumbency
being vacant. The vicarage may be empty for months, the
floor by the front door being littered with circulars and
an odd letter (if not already swept away by a cleaner).

Unless the beginner has prepared himself, he may be
disappointed when he first sees a parish register, because
he finds he cannot read the earlier entries. The hands
of the 16th and 17th century and even the 18th are
difficult to decipher until one is accustomed to them.
Photo-print copies of wills or other documents could be
obtained and studied at leisure instead of at a repository
which may be distant from home. A book such as
Examples of Handwriting, 1550-1650 or *Examples of
English Handwriting** will be found useful. The latter
reproduces documents photographically and includes a
printed transcript of each. Similar help may be found from
the will and inventory on Plates 7 and 8 of this book and
their transcripts on facing pages. It will be found that by
comparing letters of unknown words with those of words
which are obvious, the alphabet in use can gradually be
built up. Although, perhaps, more care was taken in
writing in days of old, there was good and bad writing
then just as there is today, and, even when some knowledge of the letters used has been acquired, it may take
time to become accustomed to individual handwriting.
The genealogist should always carry a pocket magnifying
glass to help him to decipher letters which are difficult,
covered by blots or faint from age.

The arrangement of a parish register will not always
be found orderly. Baptisms and burials may be inter-

*See Chapter Thirteen.

mixed and in the earlier days marriages too may be found in the same sequence. Sometimes facing pages will be used as a means of separation, sometimes opposite ends of the volume (so don't forget to look at the back end!). Volumes do not usually end completely at a fixed date. If the pages allotted to baptisms are filled, the incumbent may have started a new book for them but continued the entry of marriages and burials in the old book.

Even when separation is attempted, a stray item may be in the wrong place. In examining the registers of a parish from which the marriages had been printed, I found a marriage in amongst the burials which had not been found by the editor of the printed volume. A series of pages which appears to be blank should be carefully examined. It may be that two or three pages in the middle have been used.

One must remember, too, that the registers were sometimes kept on loose sheets which were bound up afterwards, when the sheets may have been sewn up in the wrong order. If there is no date at the top of the page, this may be very confusing. Pages should be checked to see that they are in proper serial order.

It was not uncommon for the incumbent to go round to private houses for baptisms, sometimes to baptize several infants in one house. He made his records on slips of paper, which may not have been copied into the register—such slips have been found at the bottom of the parish chest. Entries in the register, moreover, were often made weekly, and it was not difficult to forget to make one, as anybody knows who tries to make up his diary two or three days late. Sometimes the parish clerk kept the entries in a notebook, and entries have been found in such a book which are not in the official register.

Parish registers are not necessarily conclusive evidence that an infant grew up to be an adult, as burials are sometimes missing. This may, perhaps, explain some of the cases of unusual longevity. A son John is baptized, say in 1700, and dies in the same year, the burial record being omitted. Ten, or even 20 years later another son is baptised with the same name (quite common, and in early days was not unusual even when the first was still alive) and survives. His burial appearing in, say, 1800, may be related to the first baptism in error. It may be that only a will, naming sons in order of seniority, brings the error to light.

It must not be forgotten that quite often the first child was baptized (and even buried when dying in infancy) in the mother's parish. A bride dying young may also be found buried in the parish of her childhood.

In the parish register will sometimes be found more than the bare records of names. The parish of a stranger, a description such as 'widow', a man's trade, given perhaps to distinguish two of the same name, all provide valuable evidence. A list of seatholders is quite common and may sometimes be useful as evidence that a particular man was still in the parish at its date. A record of 'briefs' sometimes found may serve a similar purpose. These 'briefs' were a royal direction for contributions to some specific worthy object and have been described as 'almost an early equivalent of the Mansion House Fund or "This week's good cause" '.* The contributions received were sometimes entered in full detail in the registers. A variety of other records and notes will be found, mostly of historical, rather than genealogical, interest.

Spelling will be found to be very erratic in the registers. Entries were often made by the parish clerk who spelt more or less phonetically: perhaps, too, he was sometimes a little deaf! One must remember that education (if

The Parish Chest (Tate).

reading and writing may be called education) is a product of a later age, and that in the 17th and 18th century there were comparatively few in a village who could read and write. On reference to the register entries on Plate 1, such words as Willam, Robord, Marey will be seen. If there are such mistakes in spelling with common Christian names, it is not surprising that surnames get distorted. For instance, 'Lafenton' on that page should, judging from baptism records elsewhere in the register, probably be 'Lavington'. It was, however, not ignorance only that was responsible; spelling, up to about the end of the 18th century, just did not matter. All varieties of a surname must therefore be taken together, though they should in each case be copied in the exact spelling found. In my own case I have come across Willis, Willes, Wyllys, Willys, Wilis, Willowes, Willice or Wilce, all obviously referring to the same name. It is quite possible that sometimes the name has been written as Wills, but I have only followed up that name where there should be a likelihood of connection.

In reading parish registers one must remember the method of dating before the present-day calendar came into force in 1752. There used to be two methods of dating: one that of the Church and the legal world began the year at the Feast of Annunciation (i.e., Lady Day, 25 March), the other, used for historical purposes, beginning on 1 January. Consequently, an entry in a parish register of say, 3 February 1723, would be February in the historical year 1724 and in pedigrees and other present-day references should be described as 3 February 1723/4. As from 1 January 1752, the year began for all purposes on 1 January.* Reference to an extract from a register reproduced on Plate 1 will show

*24 Geo. II, c. 23.

where the changes in the year came. For instance, consecutive entries are dated December 1742 and January 1742/3.

Parish registers are probably the most important source of genealogical information and the first to be examined after the General Register Office and Census Returns have been disposed of. Sometimes, however, they are not conclusive by themselves. Confusion may arise where two identical names appear in the same parish (they may or may not be brothers of the same Christian name). Baptisms in later years usually give the name of father and mother, so a 'John, son of John and Alice X' will be known to be of a different family from 'Peter, son of John and Mary X'. If, however, the mother's name is not given in the register, as is often the case with early entries, and they merely appear as 'John, son of John X' and 'Peter, son of John X' there is nothing to separate the families. Here comes the value of wills, though, as will be seen in Chapter 6, the making of wills was not so common in olden days as it is today.

A grandfather's will may refer to his son John and his children Peter, James and Henry, whereas another may refer to son John and his children, John, George and Alice. Baptisms of all will quite possibly have appeared in the same register but the wills sort out the families. The will, of course, need not necessarily be the grandfather's, it might be that of any relation.

Where registers are missing or gaps appear, enquiry should be made as to the existence of the 'Bishops' Transcripts' referred to above.* Although the Bishops' Transcripts are archives of the Diocesan Registry, in most dioceses they will be found deposited elsewhere. They may be at the County Record Office. If not, the County Archivist will be able to confirm where they are.

*A complete guide to the location of parish registers will be found in *The Phillimore Atlas and Index of Parish Registers* (1984).

The transcripts may be in bundles by years rather than arranged by parishes; if so, a good deal of time may be needed to search one particular parish over a number of years. Particulars and location of these transcripts are given in the *National Index of Parish Registers* in course of publication in several volumes.* For counties not yet published in this series reference may be made to Gibson's *Bishops' Transcripts and Marriage Licences* which is a guide to their location together with other useful information. This will show from what varying dates the transcripts start, so again one may or may not be lucky. In some dioceses there may be detailed lists, such as the *Handlist of Leicestershire Parish Register Transcripts* (City of Leicester Department of Archives). Transcripts of some registers of consular offices and Anglican chaplaincies abroad were sent to the London diocese and are now in Guildhall Library, London, who publish a list.

Even if the parish registers have been seen, it is as well to see the bishops' transcript, if available, when some expected entry cannot be found. Entries have been discovered in the transcripts which do not appear in the registers, which seems to indicate that the parson sometimes kept a rough list or book and did not enter up the register till after he had sent in the transcript.

The parish registers are, of course, those of the established Church of England. Though Nonconformists (or Dissenters) were not regular members of the established Church, they still, in their earlier days at any rate, were often baptized or married there, and the right of a parishioner to be buried in the churchyard of his parish, where there is one in use, still remains, even though he may not be a member of the Church of England.

At the beginning of registration in 1837 nonconformist bodies were asked to send their registers to the Registrar

*See Chapter Thirteen.

General, and these are kept available by the P.R.O. A list
of them (officially called 'non-parochial registers') has been
published* and may be seen there, or will be found in some
of the principal libraries. It will be seen that, generally
speaking, the Roman Catholic and Jewish denominations
did not do this, and their records must be looked for elsewhere. Moreover, there was no doubt neglect by others of
the request, so that there is no guarantee that there are
none extant in other places.

The Catholic Record Society has published certain
Roman Catholic registers and the Huguenot Society of
London some of those of French Protestants in this
country. Some useful articles have been written on both
the Huguenot and Jewish problem.† If no record can be
found from any of the above sources, inquiry should be
made from the present authority of the denomination in
the locality concerned as to whether any old records
survive in their custody. The Society of Friends (Quakers)
have their own central repository of records at The
Friends' House, Euston Road, London, N.W., which
should be visited by anybody following ancestors of that
persuasion. Though their registers should be with the non-
parochial registers at the P.R.O., the Society made copies
before surrendering them.

When the possibilities of parish registers have been
exhausted, the most valuable source of information will
be the record of wills and administrations. But, whilst
the opportunity is there, examination should be made of
other parish documents which will be found kept with the
registers or otherwise in the charge of the incumbent.

---

*List of Non-parochial Registers in the Custody of the Registrar
General.* H.M.S.O. 1859.

†*Huguenot Records.* S. Minet. *The Genealogists' Magazine*, xxi,
p. 149 (1956). *My Ancestor was Jewish.* Society of Genealogists
(1982). Also *National Index of Parish Registers*, Vol. 3, and (for
Nonconformists) Vol. 2.

Something will be said of the value of these in the next chapter before dealing with the subject of wills.

In concluding the chapter on parish registers the attention of the searcher must be drawn to the valuable aid now provided by the International Genealogical Index ('Mormon microfiche'), especially useful when losing track of a family in one particular parish. This Index is available at the Guildhall Library, London, the Society of Genealogists, and at some local record offices. (For further details see pp. 70-71).

Chapter Five

OTHER PARISH RECORDS

THE MAJORITY of surviving parish records, other than the registers, are either concerned with the administration of Church funds or with the responsibility of the parish to the poor.

The general expense accounts of churchwardens are not likely to help much with the proof of a pedigree, but they often mention names of those to whom payment is made, and some information may be gathered of their status accordingly.

The records of rates levied are more useful. From quite early times the parishioners assembled as a 'vestry' had the power to levy a church rate for maintenance of the church fabric or other such purpose: later they were also responsible for making a rate to support the poor. The rate book of the parish, where surviving, will be found to record the names of parishioners and their assessments, so providing, like the lists of seatholders sometimes found in the registers, useful evidence of who was in the parish at the time and giving some idea of their substance. An example will be seen in a later chapter of a valuable genealogical clue given by rate books.*

However, perhaps the most valuable parish records for the genealogist, after the registers, are the 'settlement certificates' (*see* Plate 4), sometimes found amongst parish papers, because by them can be proved the removal of a family, often otherwise very difficult to trace. These

*See pages 172-173.

certificates were a result of the increasing burden of the poor on a parish. An Act of 1601* laid down that overseers were to be appointed to act with the churchwardens in maintaining the poor and providing them with work, and in 1662 another Act† gave authority for removal of a stranger to his own parish unless he rented a property of the value of £10. It was by an Act of 1697‡ that the system of settlement certificates was established. A poor man was very restricted in his movements and was liable to be sent back to his own parish to be maintained there, if the necessity arose. He could acquire a settlement in a new parish under certain conditions, but, if he looked like being a charge on the parish, the authorities naturally did all they could to prevent a settlement. They had power to require him to obtain from his own parish a certificate that he was settled there, such certificate giving an undertaking to receive him back. These certificates were carefully kept as the authority for returning a man, and by that chance it has become sometimes easier to trace the movements of a poor family than those of the more prosperous classes. With the certificates may sometimes be found records of the declaration of their circumstances which these men had to make and such records often give information of family descent.** Removal orders arising from the settlement certificates are also sometimes found.

Since the churchwardens and overseers were responsible for putting the poor to work they were often parties to apprenticeship deeds. They were empowered to place apprentices with the consent of the justices, and indentures may be found with the parish documents, again throwing

*43 Eliz. I, c.2.
†14 Car. II, c.12.
‡8 and 9 W. and M., c. 30.
**See *Winchester Settlement Papers 1667-1842.* Arthur J. Willis, 1967.

light on the movement of the poorer members of the
community. In some cases a borough would undertake
the placing of apprentices.*

Records of marriage licences† may sometimes be
found, particularly where the incumbent was a surrogate
for granting licences. Their value is obvious.

Tithe maps are parish records but, as there should
be a copy with the episcopal records in the charge of
the Diocesan Registrar, they are mentioned below under
Ecclesiastical Records.‡

A great variety of other documents may be found from
incumbents' diaries to certificates for touching for the
King's evil (i.e., a certificate from the minister and church-
wardens that a sufferer from scrofula had not before
received the Royal touch which was supposed to cure it).
When the parish of the family whose genealogy is being
traced has been ascertained, all documents in the parish
chest or vestry cupboard should be examined for possible
evidence. This may mean spending a long time, as there
are not likely to be indexes, but it is a 'must'. In many
cases all such documents may have been transferred to
the County Record Office, so enquiry may well be made
there first.

*See *A Calendar of Southampton Apprenticeship Registers,
1609-1740*. Arthur J. Willis and A. L. Merson   (Southampton
Records Series, 1968).

†See page 88.

‡See page 93.

Twentieth day of July one Thousand Seven Hundred and Seventy Six

Know all Men by these Presents that I Richard Whitmaich a Minor of the Age of ten years or thereabouts one of the natural and lawful Children and also eldest Son and Heir at Law of Richard Whitmaich late of the parish of Whippingham in the Isle of Wight in the County of Southampton and (Diocese) of Winchester Yeoman deced Have made authorized appointed and chosen and by these Presents DO make authorize appoint and chose my beloved Mother Elizabeth Whitmaich Widow relict of my said late Father Richard Whitmaich deced to be my true and lawful Guardian or Curator to take care of and receive to and for my Use and Benefit during my Minority all and every such Monies Rents and arrears of Rent (if any) Issues and profits which I am by reason of the Death of my said late Father interested in or intitled to from by and out of the Rents Copyhold and Personal Estate or Estates he was by Virtue of the last Will and Testament of Richard Whitmaich late of Newport aforesaid Yeoman deced or otherwise howsoever interested in or intitled unto And for me to give and execute any Release or other proper Discharges for the same And that this my Proxy or nomination of Guardian or Curator may have due effect in Law Ido hereby impower and authorize Richard Holloway Notary public one of the Proctors General of the Consistory Court of the Lord Bishop of Winchester to be my true and lawful Proctor for me and in my Name to appear before the Worshipful George Harris Clerk Dr of Laws Vicar General and Official Principal of the Right Reverend Father in God John by Divine Permission Lord Bishop of Winchester or his lawful Surrogate or any other competent Judge in this Behalf and to exhibit this my Proxy and to pray and procure the same to be admitted and enacted and generally to do all other Acts and Things in this behalf necessary to be done and executed hereby ratifying and confirming all and whatsoever my said Proctor shall lawfully do or cause to be done in the Premises by Virtue of these presents In Witness whereof I have hereunto set my Hand and Seal this (Day and Year first above written)

Sealed and delivered (being first
duly stampt) in the presence of)

Richard Whitmaich

Leigh Frattle

Plate 2. A Guardianship Appointment.
(Reproduced by courtesy of the Hampshire Record Office)

Chapter Six

WILLS AND ADMINISTRATIONS

BEFORE 1858 WILLS were a matter for ecclesiastical authority. Early wills will be found nearly always opening with a prayer for the testator's soul, committal of his body to the churchyard of his parish, sometimes followed by a legacy to the Church, before attention is turned to secular matters. The will was proved in the Court of the archdeacon or bishop within whose archdeaconry or diocese respectively the property was held, except where some incumbent or other authority had 'peculiar' jurisdiction excluding these Courts. Where property was held in more than one archdeaconry of a diocese the will had to be proved in the Bishop's Court, if in more than one diocese in the Prerogative Court of the Province—i.e., Canterbury or York. The exact rules deciding which was the proper Court in which to prove a will are now rather obscure, as there were periods during a 'visitation' when one minor Court was 'inhibited' and recourse must be had to a superior authority. The above general rule will, however, give a guide as to where to look first. If a particular will is not found where it may be expected, the possibility of a Superior Court should be examined.

During the Commonwealth from about 1652 to 1660 ecclesiastical jurisdiction in the matter of wills was suspended and all wills had to be proved before a civil authority in London. On the Restoration jurisdiction was resumed by the Church.

By the Court of Probate Act of 1857* the Principal Probate Registry was established in London with a number

*20 & 21 Vic., c. 77

of District Registries subordinated to it, and the Church was finally deprived of the jurisdiction. The Church records of wills should have been taken over by the Probate Registry in or near each diocese and kept there available ever since. Such wills have now mostly been handed over to other authorities, such as County Record Offices. At the P.R.O. are the records of the Prerogative Court of Canterbury which incorporate the record during the Commonwealth period referred, to above. The records of the Prerogative Court of York are deposited with the Borthwick Institute of Historical Research at York.

In such Church records will be found original wills (or copies) filed according to date of probate. In some cases 'Probate Act Books' may be available in which are entered all the probates granted. For some periods, too, there may be volumes of 'registered copies', i.e., volumes in which the wills have been transcribed in full as each was proved, often with the probate act following it. Practically the whole period for which wills are extant in the Prerogative Courts is covered by such registered copies bound up in large volumes.

Where there was no will or some irregularity in it, letters of administration, commonly referred to as 'admons.', were granted, as they are today. The bonds entered into by the administrators may be found available in some cases and, just as for probates, there may be an (Admon.) Act Book. Admon. may be granted with the will annexed, if, for example, no executor is named or the executor has renounced or died before completing distribution of the estate.

With both proved wills and admons. it will often be found, particularly in the earlier cases, that an inventory is filed with the papers; sometimes an inventory may be there and the will missing, but the admon. may be endorsed on the inventory. The gaps in wills are many, but one must remember that there was not the necessity in

the 16th and 17th century for a will that there is now.
Many were tenants of a manor, so had no real estate to
dispose of: there were none of the registered securities
that there are today, which need proof of title before a
transfer can be made. Property was mostly portable and no
doubt the family divided the farm stock, furniture, etc.,
according to the known wishes of the deceased or by
mutual agreement between themselves. In early days there
was little means of investment for cash, except perhaps
money lent on a bond, so pecuniary legacies were few.

Volumes of MS. indexes will be found in each repository which purport to show all wills and admons. filed: in
some cases these have been printed, a new index being
usually made from the Act Book or original documents.
Unfortunately, sometimes wills recorded as existing cannot
be traced and some may be found which are not indexed.
The MS. indexes have mostly been prepared in the 17th
or 18th century and documents have no doubt from time
to time been displaced. A certain number of calendars of
wills and admons. have been printed by the British Record
Society or local record societies, and it is advisable to find
out whether those of the Court under consideration have
been printed and until what date, as in many cases those
of the 18th and 19th centuries have not yet been fully
covered. If found, reference will be easier, and the wills
required can be picked out before making a journey to
the repository.

In the case of wills proved since 1858 (when the Court
of Probate was established), a search should be made in
the Probate Court Indexes at Somerset House, London.
When reference to a required will has been found a
registered copy will be produced on payment of a small
fee. It is a help to know the date of death—at least
approximately—as the indexes are arranged alphabetically
for each year. In the case of a common surname the
searcher should, of course, be able to identify the particular

will by Christian name and place of death. Copies of wills may be obtained, and, if date of death is known, ordered by post at a cost of 25p per page plus handling charge of £1. Applications should be addressed to the Record Keeper, Correspondence Department, Somerset House, Strand, London WC2R 1LA.

In the case of wills proved before 1858, these will have been proved in the Ecclesiastical Courts, generally speaking either:

The Prerogative Court of the Province (Canterbury or York).
The Bishop's Court of a Diocese.
An Archdeacon's Court of a Diocese.
A Court having 'Peculiar' jurisdiction.

It is advisable to know the date and place of death of the testator whose will is being searched for. If the place is known the will should be looked for in the Indexes of the Bishop's Court of the Diocese, and the relative Archdeacon's Court or, if it appears from the list of 'Peculiars' in the Diocese that one of these may have had jurisdiction, the Index of Peculiar Courts should be examined. Failing these, the Prerogative Court list of the Province should be searched, where the will would have been proved if the testator owned property in more than one diocese. Wills proved during the Commonwealth whilst the authority of the Ecclesiastical Courts was suspended will be found in the indexes of the Prerogative Court of Canterbury.

There is a helpful guide* in searching for wills before 1858: *A Simplified Guide to Probate Jurisdiction* (J. S. W.

Wills and Where to Find Them (J. S. W. Gibson, 1974) and *Wills and Their Whereabouts* (A. J. Camp, 1974) are now out of print.

Gibson, 1982). This book covers Great Britain and
Ireland, and its purpose is to suggest where to start looking
for wills. The arrangement of the book is by county and
thereunder by court of jurisdiction and repository, with
information indicating present location of wills, period of
coverage and existence of indexes.

Having studied this guide to find out which was
the court having jurisdiction in the locality concerned,
one will have to visit the appropriate repository which will
have an index of names and produce the documents. In
some cases there will be published lists which can be
examined beforehand. It should not be forgotten that if a
will cannot be found there may be an admon. (usually
listed separately) which may give some information on
next of kin.

Something further should be said about P.C.C wills
at the Public Record Office. For such registered wills
(PROB. 11) one must be prepared with a year and folio
reference from the index books (PROB. 12). Up to 1700
indexes have been published, mostly in the Index Library
publications.* There reference is in the form of a volume
covered by the book and the year of each.† The class list
of the P.R.O. will give a reference number for each volume
of registered wills. Some years are in more than one
volume, so the list will also give the folios covered by the
volume in question, e.g.:—

Prob. 11	*Date*	*Name of register*	*Folio Nos.*
70	1587	Spencer	1-40

If, therefore, one is looking for Spencer 34, which one has

*The Society of Genealogists have a series 1750-1800 in progress
and have published initials A—C (part).

†A complete list of volume names and year dates will be found in
Genealogical Research in England and Wales, vol. 2, pp. 91-2.

ascertained to be a volume of 1587, the reference to be given will be PROB. 11/70, for which folios 1-40 would be produced. It will be found that the 'folio' reference is actually to a number of leaves in the volume (not a single leaf as one might expect), so that one will have to look through a section of, perhaps, 12 pages to find the required will (the reference is marked on the first page of the section).

P.C.C. original wills (PROB. 10) and inventories (PROB. 2-5) are also available, but it would probably be simplest and satisfactory to see the registered copy in the first instance. Some special reason, such as to see a signature, may make it necessary to see the original. Inventories are of historical rather than genealogical interest, but throw light on the occupation and condition of the family.

P.C.C. Administrations (PROB. 6 and 7) will be found in separate volumes known as Act Books. These are books of entry recording the grants of administration. There are similar probate act books, but these are not normally needed as a copy of the probate act is usually appended to the registered copy of the will.

Both registered copies and original wills as well as act books are in contemporary hands, so the searcher, as in the case of parish registers, must be prepared to decipher the old script. Registered copies are in a formal legible hand, but originals may be very roughly written. In studying handwriting full use should be made of those publications which reproduce handwriting in facsimile with transcription.* These soon familiarise one with the style, but there will always be bad writing as there is today.

If a will required has been found in a printed calendar, enquiry might be made of the repository whether there is a professional searcher locally who can make an abstract, so that a journey can be saved. One should remember that

*see Chapter Thirteen.

professional help is not restricted to complete pedigree
searching, but can be used for one particular inspection to
instructions. It is advisable to enquire as to fees and agree
them beforehand.

When examining wills one can either make an abstract
or order a photoprint, which most record offices can
supply.

The amount of information obtainable from wills varies
considerably. In some of the more ancient ones the testator sometimes aggravatingly refers to relationships without
giving names, or to 'kinsmen' without giving relationship.
He may leave everything to one person or make the
genealogist rub his hands with glee by mentioning all the
members of a large family including 'his sisters, his
cousins and his aunts'. One would naturally search first
for the family name but almost equally important may be
the wills of 'in-laws'—a father-in-law or mother-in-law
(being a widow)* may well leave property to the family
and particularly mention grandchildren: uncles and aunts,
too, may mention their nephews and nieces, great-nephews
and great-nieces. The names of families allied by marriage
should be noted for this purpose.

In the will on pages 154-5 Ann Penton and Elizabeth
Jestis are daughters and their children named George and
Peter respectively are entered in the pedigree on Chart 1.
Their line is not pursued as they have left the Willis family
and name.

One must not forget that until the Married Women's
Property Act of 1882† the property of a married woman
was with some exceptions, such as property held under a
settlement, that of her husband, and that, therefore, if
she predeceased her husband she could normally leave
no will. Once she was widowed, she could, of course, dispose of property.

*Father, etc. '-in-law' may mean 'step-father', etc.
†45 and 46 Vic. c.75.

When a will required has been found, an abstract of it should be made on a separate sheet for filing as suggested in Chapter 3. The following information should always be noted:

Name of testator.
Occupation and/or address (in old wills probably only the parish), if given.
Date of execution of the will.
Place of burial desired (this may indicate a family move).
Names and relationship of all beneficiaries.
Particulars of all landed estate mentioned.
Names of executors, supervisors and overseers (if any).
Names of witnesses.
Particulars of heraldic seal (if any).
Date and place of probate.
Where the will was seen, whether it was the original or a copy, and the repository's reference number.

In individual cases there may be some special mention which should be recorded. For instance, the articles bequeathed may be of family interest though not material evidence genealogically. It may be mentioned that it is common in a will to see a legacy of one shilling (*see* Plate 7). This is not an example of the popular phrase 'cutting him off with a shilling'. It is usually included to indicate that the individual is not forgotten, where he has had his portion, perhaps, in the testator's lifetime.

Nor must it be assumed where administration is granted to a creditor, the widow renouncing, that the testator was necessarily bankrupt. It may be merely a means of preventing a rush of small creditors who would eat up the estate.

It must not be forgotten that a will reflects conditions at the time of its execution, not at the time of death. If some years have elapsed, children born in the interval will not be mentioned by name (though the possibility of their birth may be provided for in anticipation). Legatees, too, or others mentioned in the will may have predeceased the testator.

A few of the key words used in probate and admon. acts may be mentioned:

The probate act usually begins with the word 'Probatum', which shows at once that a will was proved, the word not being used for admons. (with or without a will).

The grant in both probate and admon. acts is expressed as 'admio (administratio) commissa fuit . . .'

The relationship in the case of admons. is usually given, e.g., 'fratri, sorori, matri', 'nepoti ex filia' (a grandson by the daughter, i.e., a grandson who is a daughter's son), 'nepoti ex fratre' (a nephew).

The date is mostly written in words, but the year may be expressed in the normal Arabic numerals (though often only in words), so a knowledge of the Latin words for numerals is valuable. In early wills the year is expressed in Roman numerals, which may cause some difficulty. It should be noted that the last i in Roman figures is written as a j, e.g. viij = 8.

The date, when between 1 January and 24 March, may be followed by 'juxta &c.'* or 'stylo Angl.' These terms mean that the year is reckoned as beginning on 25 March. For example, such a reference after 16 January 1720 would mean 1720/21.

The month may be abbreviated to 9ber (November), 8ber (October).

Estate Duty Wills

At one time there was a duty payable on legacies varying with the relationship of the legatee and abstracts

*See pages 154-155.

of wills were for this reason deposited with the Stamp Office.

These abstracts were destroyed, but the registers (IR 26) giving names of executors, legatees, amounts of duty payable etc. exist and are now available from 1796 to 1903. There are no later ones. Until 1812 they cover a very small percentage of estates. All courts are covered. Indexes (IR 27) and registers are available in the Wills Room at the P.R.O., Chancery Lane.*

The possibilities of parish records, census returns and wills, the leading sources, being exhausted, one must consider the great variety of other sources which might help, and decide which is the most likely. Much will depend on the status of the family. In the case of the nobility and gentry printed books may help, as there are printed pedigrees, family histories and other printed records of leading families. There is also a vast mass of public records in which reference may be found both to the gentry and to the ordinary people. Let us, therefore, consider next the possibilities of the Public Record Office and the use of libraries.

*See P.R.O. leaflet 34.

Chapter Seven

THE PUBLIC RECORD OFFICE

THE PUBLIC RECORD OFFICE is the repository of official records of either the Courts of Law or of the Departments of State. For the genealogist it is only in so far as his quarry has come into contact with such official bodies that he will find mention of him there. If he was a litigant or delinquent, or, as a member of the Navy or Army or otherwise, was of interest to a Government Department, there may be information about him in the Public Records. Taxation may have brought him to the notice of the Exchequer or transfer of landed property to the Court of Chancery. The mass of material is enormous, and only a few of the more obvious and important sources of information will be mentioned.* These will probably be the first to be investigated unless a definite clue leads elsewhere. If so, its particular direction should be followed; unless there is some such guidance the searcher may find himself lost in a maze of lists, indexes and calendars if he strays beyond the few recognised sources of genealogical information. An examination of the *Guide to the Contents of the Public Record Office* will give an idea of the immense variety of material. To take just two items, a very small bite out of the whole, there are 17,471 volumes of Ships' Musters for the period 1688-1808 in the Admiralty records and 13,305 volumes of Muster Books (General) amongst the War Office records.

*See P.R.O. leaflet 37; *Genealogy from the Public Records* and J. Cox and T. Padfield, *Tracing your Ancestors in the Public Record Office* (H.M.S.O., 1983).

Applications for permission to use the Search Rooms must be made to the Keeper of Public Records, by whom a student's ticket will be issued on his being satisfied as to the *bona fides* and responsibility of the applicant. There is no fee.*

The Public Record Office is now divided into two main parts, one at Kew (which is now regarded as the headquarters), and the other in Chancery Lane, London. Generally speaking, the more ancient records have been retained at the old office in London, while the more modern records have been removed to the repository beside the Thames at Kew.

KEW

Although the records most likely to interest beginners still remain in London, mention may be made of some classes now deposited at Kew.

The address of this repository is Ruskin Avenue, Kew, Richmond, Surrey TW9 4DU, (telephone 01-876-3444). It is open Monday to Friday 9.30 to 5 p.m. except the usual public holidays, and two weeks closure for stock-taking some time around the beginning of October. The nearest station is Kew Gardens, whence there is a walk of about 10 minutes. There are, in addition, several bus-stops in the vicinity, and ample space at the Record Office for car-parking. It is recommended that those intending to visit the Search Rooms at Kew should first write for an information leaflet and guide map.

A reader's ticket may be obtained at the counter in the vast entrance hall, reminiscent of an airport lounge. (The same ticket can be used for Chancery Lane, and

---

*Day-passes will be issued to those who only wish to consult indexes.

for the Census Room in Portugal Street.) The main search room and reference room, equally spacious, are on the first floor.

Documents are ordered by means of computer, six terminals for this purpose being available in the Reference Room. But before going there it is advisable to apply for a seat number and pocket-'bleeper' at the desk in the Search Room, as the seat number will be required when tapping out requests for documents on the computer. All the necessary lists, indexes and reference books are to be found on the shelves in the Reference Room, and those who may feel somewhat at sea in this 'brave new world' will find the staff most helpful and sympathetic.*

Having ordered the documents required, one can wander round, possibly having lunch at the reasonably priced restaurant or eat one's own sandwich in the basement, and wait for the bleeper to bleep (at least, theoretically). This is a sign that the documents are waiting to be collected at the desk in the Search Room. There is a further search room on the second floor, intended for maps and large documents: the computer screen should indicate whether the document is to be produced in the Map Room.

The following classes of document are those most likely to be of interest to the genealogist:

Apprenticeship Books

Owing to the obligation to pay a stamp duty on apprenticeship indentures, there are, with the records of the Inland Revenue, a series of Apprenticeship Books covering a period from 1710 to 1811 (IR 1). These are of value as they contain an entry of each apprenticeship, giving the name of the apprentice, the name and trade of the master and sometimes name of father and the place of residence

*For a useful article on ordering by computer at Kew, see *The Genealogists' Magazine*, vol. 19, No. 7 (Sep. 1978) pp. 249-251.

of each. A typescript index of names in these books with brief particulars of the apprenticeship has been made up to 1774 which can be consulted at the Library of the Society of Genealogists. There is with it an Index of Apprentice Masters up to 1762 which is sometimes useful.

Professional Records

The professions associated with the Departments of State or the Courts will have records at the P.R.O. (see also below under 'Chancery Lane').

Army*

Printed Army Lists are available from 1754 (WO 65-66) and there are MS. lists from 1702 (WO 64). Some of these can, of course, be seen in certain Libraries, but the P.R.O. series will be more complete.

Muster Books (WO 10-15) which begin in 1708 list both officers and other ranks by regiments. It is, therefore, essential that the regiment should be known before searching. In the case of an officer, if it is not known, it may be found from the printed Army List. These books will usually give at the man's first muster his age and place of birth.

There are Description Books 1765-1900 (WO 25) and 1768-1908 (WO 67) which give a description of soldiers and usually state their date and place of birth.

Militia records 1759-1925 (WO 68) include some registers of births and marriages and there are militia attestation papers 1806-1915 (WO 96).

Navy†

Printed Navy Lists can be seen from 1799.

Ships' Musters are available 1688-1878 (Adm. 36-39) and Ships Pay Books 1669-1832 (Adm. 31-35). Just as in

*See P.R.O. leaflet 9.

†See P.R.O. leaflet 18.

the Army regiments must be known, so here the name of
the ship must be known to enable an individual member of
the crew to be traced.

Lieutenants' Passing Certificates 1691-1848 (Adm. 107)
will usually have baptism records.

There are some Supplementary Papers (Adm. 13) which
include further Lieutenants' Passing Certificates and some
marriage certificates 1806-1902; also seamen's wills (ADM
48 and 142).

Naturalization Certificates (HO 1)

Lists may be seen at Chancery Lane but the actual
documents are at Kew. Information varies but would
probably give place of residence, whether married or
unmarried, occupation and country of origin.

Tithe Maps*

Tithe Maps (IR 30) and Tithe Apportionments (IR 29)
which give schedules of names of owners and occupiers
will be produced in the Map Room (P.R.O. leaflet 13).

CHANCERY LANE

The opening hours are the same as for the office at Kew
(see above). Application for a ticket should be made at
the enquiry office, and the ticket, once obtained, is valid
at all branches of the P.R.O.

There are two search rooms on the ground floor: the
Round Room and the Long Room. Generally speaking,
reference books, lists and indexes on the shelves in the
Round Room refer to earlier records, while those in the
Long Room predominantly refer to legal records. Type-
writers may be used at certain tables in the Long Room,

*See page 93.

where there is also an ultra-violet reader for MSS. which are difficult to decipher. On the ground floor is also the Photographic Department, where photocopies of documents may be ordered.

On the first floor is the Wills Room, where P.C.C. Wills are produced, and where indexes both to them and to Estate Duty Wills are to be found. Beyond this is the North Room, reserved for large documents.

Kew lists, printed indexes to wills and various standard reference books, also Boyd's Marriage Index, are available at Chancery Lane.

A series of Class Lists is available in the Search Rooms which classify the whole of the records within the Department of State or the Court to which they refer, with sub-classification according to the nature of the documents. These Class Lists give reference numbers of index volumes (of which there are several thousand). It may not be necessary to refer to these indexes, as many categories have been listed or calendared, sometimes even with an index of names or places. From these the reference required for production of the document can be found. Inside the entrance to the Round Room is a card index which gives particulars of lists and indexes for each category of the records and where they may be found.

A simple system of reference to the many thousands of documents has been evolved. The index volume referred to usually has its letter reference given on the inside of the front cover. An Index of Chancery Proceedings has, perhaps, a reference C8 and a particular item is given a reference 94/153 (i.e., item 153 in bundle 94). The only reference required to trace the particular document is C8 94/153. This being filled in on a slip, the document will be looked out and produced usually within half an hour to an hour.

Some useful leaflets are available at the P.R.O. on records of interest to genealogists, such as births, marriages and deaths, census, probate, immigrants, emigrants, military service, etc.

Some records are kept at Hayes, Middlesex, and may only be inspected by prior appointment.

Something will now be said about each of a few main items of interest to the genealogist.

Wills

The subject of P.C.C. wills and Estate Duty Wills has already been dealt with in the Wills chapter.

Non-Parochial Registers

The non-parochial registers have already been referred to on page 36. Lists are in the Long Room.

Professional Records

Solicitors and attorneys

A Reference Guide on the subject is available in the Long Room.

Clergy

Most records of clergy will be in the dioceses, but there is a series of Institution Books (1556-1838), based on certificates of institution of incumbents returned to the Exchequer for collection of 'first fruits and tenths'.

Lay Subsidies

Amongst Exchequer records are the Subsidy Rolls, which include assessments and accounts for various grants made to the Crown, by Convocation for the Clergy and by the House of Commons for laity. The latter, the 'lay subsidies', which extend up to the time of Charles II

(E. 179), are useful to genealogists as they give the names of those who contribute. They are listed by years and hundred divisions of the county, so if the locality is known rolls of the appropriate hundred could be examined. With them is included the hearth tax of Charles II's reign.*

With the lists of lay subsidy rolls are indexes of 'certificates of residence'. These are in effect certificates that somebody assessed had removed from the locality, and so were a kind of voucher for non-payment of the lay subsidies. They extend from the time of Elizabeth I to that of Charles II and the indexes are of names in alphabetical order with the county given.

The lists of both lay subsidy rolls and certificates of residence are on the shelves of the Round Room.

Manorial Records

A certain number of manorial court records are in the P.R.O., but the subject will be dealt with in a later chapter.†

Royalist Composition Papers

Where landowners had during the Civil War supported the King against the Commonwealth their lands were confiscated by order of Committees appointed to investigate the action of the owners. The owners, having confessed their 'delinquency' and given a pledge to adhere to the Commonwealth, had to give a full account of their possessions and were then allowed to 'compound' by surrendering a proportion of their estate which varied according to their guilt. The records of these Committees, therefore, give a good deal of information about the condition of such individuals, often mentioning their heirs and other members of their family.

*14 Car. II, c.10.

† See page 95.

'Inquisitions Post-Mortem'

Information which the manorial roll gives as to succession of tenants of a manor, the *inquisitio post mortem* records of tenants *in capite* of the Crown. On the death of such a tenant an inquiry was held as to the lands held by the deceased and the terms of service under which they were held, and this inquiry usually elicits the date of the tenant's death and the name, age and relationship of the next heir. Records of these inquiries are, therefore, of great genealogical value. We are, however, now getting to rather early times as these *inquisitiones post mortem* do not extend much later than the times of Charles I and are, of course, reported in Latin.

Law Court Records Generally

The records of the various Law Courts will be found at the P.R.O., so, if the family has been known to have engaged in a lawsuit, information may be found available, e.g., affidavits filed and judgements. There are, moreover, filed with Court records a number of private deeds of various kinds not referring to lawsuits.

Amongst Law Court Records should be specially mentioned:

Chancery Proceedings *

A good deal of litigation, largely in relation to property or money came before the Equity side of the Court of Chancery in the form of petitions (or 'bills') with which their answers and depositions in the suit were filed. Calendars of the early suits have been printed, but for later ones only manuscript calendars are available. These are classified under the names of the Six Clerks and up to 1714 give bundle reference number, names of plaintiffs

---

*See *Chancery and Other Legal Proceedings*, R. E. F. Garrett, (Pinhorn, 1968), and P.R.O. leaflet 32.

and defendants, date and subject matter of the suit and name of the county. The particulars are grouped under the initial letter of the principal plaintiff's name, and one may therefore find a suit where this is known. But it is not so easy to trace the name of a defendant or associated plaintiff. It is, of course, necessary to search the lists of all the Six Clerks, unless it is known by which one the suit was handled. Particularly where several members of the same family are either joint or opposite parties, relationship may be established from these suits. The lists after 1714 give names of parties only without any county, so the help of locality in eliminating the unwanted is not available. The lists are kept in the Long Room.

The value to genealogists of these proceedings is, however, not so much in the bills and answers as in the depositions of witnesses which are filed with the papers. The deponents give information as to their age and place of residence and other genealogical information might be found. A few deponents are listed in manuscript in the Library of the Society of Genealogists and the Bernau Index* gives a fuller guide. Otherwise it is difficult to find an individual deponent, unless he is known to have been concerned with some particular case.

Exchequer Depositions

Similar depositions are found taken on commission for the Court of Exchequer. There is a printed calendar and here supplementary information is available to trace deponents, as there is a typed list of deponents in each case for the period 1559-1695, the cases being arranged in groups according to locality, with the county given in a marginal heading (this will be found on the shelves of the Society of Genealogists, where there are also manuscript slips for the later period up to 40 Geo. III).

*See page 70.

Court of Requests and Star Chamber

The proceedings of these courts sometimes provide genealogical information. There are indexes of names for both of these courts on the Round Room shelves covering the Tudor period, and, in the case of the Court of Requests, also for the period of James I.

Feet of Fines*

When conveyance of landed property was in a very rudimentary stage somebody seems to have discovered that if there could be a dispute at law about the ownership of land, and that dispute was settled by the Court, first-class evidence as to ownership was provided. Hence it seems there arose the series of 'Fines' (so called because they made a final end to the dispute, the general opening of the 'Foot of Fine' being *Hec est finalis concordia . . .*'). The 'Fine' was an agreement or composition of a suit (usually fictitious) made between the parties with the consent of the Court and by which the transfer or settlement of freehold property was determined. There were several steps in the procedure, but the 'Foot of Fine' set out the terms of the agreement. Where several members of the same family were concerned, their relationship would normally be given. Feet of Fines are in Latin until the time of George II, after which they are in English.

Some indexes and calendars to Feet of Fines have been published by various local societies, and these are the easiest means of reference.

*   *   *

Some of the items mentioned above are rather approaching more advanced work, but it seems advisable to draw attention to their existence. The main interest of the

*See 'Feet of Fines', M. Tatchell, *The Genealogists' Magazine*, vol. 19 No. 10 (June 1979) pp. 347-349.

beginner at the P.R.O. will probably be in the Census records, P.C.C. Wills, the Apprenticeship Books, and perhaps Admiralty or War Office enrolments. There are, however, public records elsewhere, e.g., county and municipal archives and such semi-public records as public men's correspondence, as well as a very large number of printed books transcribing records. Other important repositories for genealogists will be the British Library and the Library of the Society of Genealogists for records of a national nature, whilst those of local interest may be found with the county or municipal or even private collections.

Next, therefore, must be examined the resources of libraries, which will cover not only manuscripts but the vast collection of printed books available.

Chapter Eight

THE SOCIETY OF GENEALOGISTS' LIBRARY

BEFORE THE SEARCHER undertakes a visit to the British Library he should first make a point of examining the shelves of the Library of the Society of Genealogists, which has a specialised collection of genealogical books and other material. The Library is at 14 Charterhouse Buildings, London EC1, within easy walking distance of Barbican Station. Membership of the Society requires an entrance fee of £7.50 ($15) and a subscription of £14.00 ($28) for country or overseas members or £20.00 for town members. This is, of course, an advantage, but non-members may use the Library on payment of a fee.* The hours of opening are: Tuesdays, Fridays and Saturdays 10-6, Wednesdays and Thursdays 10-8 (closed on Mondays).† It contains a large proportion of the recognised printed reference books (but, not quite all, as the Society was only founded in 1911 and there are still gaps).

Most of these books can be seen at the British Library or at other libraries, but it is a great advantage to have them collected together on open shelves, so that all one has to do is to take down the book and look at it without any filling-in of forms or waiting. Some of the books, such as school registers or family histories, which were privately

---

*£2.00 for an hour, £4.00 for 3½ hours, £6.00 for a day and £7.50 for a day and evening.

†For Bank Holiday periods and stocktaking make enquiry.

issued and so not supplied to the 'Copyright Libraries', also most of the manuscripts, may be difficult to find elsewhere.

The Society is able to undertake a certain amount of research for members and non-members in its own collections and elsewhere. Searches for members are at a slightly reduced rate. The Society can also give names of searchers. All correspondence should be prepaid.

There is a short guide to the Library given free to day-searchers and new members. Some detail of the manuscript collections will be found in the Genealogists' Handbook and the Society's published lists (*see* Chapter Thirteen).

A summary of the principal records available in this Library is appended.* This is obviously not exhaustive and, when a series of publications is mentioned, it must not be assumed to be complete.

Regional

There is a regional classification of England by counties, London and Middlesex being together, and there are sections covering Wales, Scotland and Ireland. The Scottish section includes microfilms of the Indexes to births, marriages and deaths at Edinburgh G.R.O. (1855–1920) and the register entries for 1855. The records in the Library include :

Parish register copies printed, typescript and manuscript.
Publications of local Record Societies.
Directories.
Poll Books.
Other local records, such as town histories, printed bishop's registers, some records of the Livery Companies of the City of London, etc.

---

*See also *Using the Library of the Society of Genealogists* (Society of Genealogists' publication).

There is a separate section for America, including many American genealogical publications, a small section for the Commonwealth and Empire (past and present), mainly relating to India, including the East India Company's Kalendars and Directories of 1794. There are a few records from foreign countries.

National Record Societies

Harleian Society.
British Record Society (Index Library).
Catholic Record Society.
Huguenot Society of London.
Society of Friends.
Camden Society.
Selden Society.
Royal Historical Society.
Naval and Military histories.

Periodicals

Navy Lists from 1798.
Army Lists from 1740.
Air Force Lists from 1938.
A few Law Lists from 1819.
Medical Directories or Registers from 1847 (London from 1845).
Dentists' Directories 1888-1922.
Clergy Lists from 1829.
Notes and Queries from 1849.
Almanac de Gotha 1821-1939.
Gentleman's Magazine 1731-1867.
Scots Magazine 1739-1802.
Monthly Magazine 1796-1812.
United Service Magazine 1857-1860.
Annual Register 1758-1813.
London Magazine 1740-1773.

The Evening Mail 1798–1818.
Genealogical Periodicals, old and new.

General Reference Books

Wills (various printed lists, the Harleian Society and British Record Society publications, also microfilms of the original will calendars of most of the local courts in England and Wales).

Marriage Licences (published lists).

Peerages, Landed Gentry and similar lists, including old issues from the 19th century.

Heraldry.

Who's Who and Who was Who.

Heralds' Visitations.

Book Plates.

Dictionary of National Biography.

Rose's Biographical Dictionary.

Annual Biography and Obituary 1817–1831.

Some Calendars of State Papers, etc., and P.R.O. printed Lists.

Historical MSS. Commission.

Topographical Dictionaries and County Histories.

Registers of the Universities and their Colleges and of the Inns of Court.

School Registers.

Family Histories

A large collection of printed or MS. volumes arranged alphabetically, also some smaller items in tract form classified separately.

Text Books

A number of text books and books on the subject of genealogy generally, or related to it, are grouped together.

Card Indexes

Great Card Index: A very large card index with, perhaps, two or three million slips, arranged by surname with reference to sources.

Other card indexes: Bloom Index (ecclesiastical).
Fawcett Index (mostly clergy of the North of England).
Glencross Index (surnames).
Glencross Index (place names).
Graham Index (mostly Scottish families).
Whitfield Index (families of Cheshire, Salop, Staffs, etc.).
Macleod Collection. Working papers of two Scottish genealogists for several hundred Scottish families (alphabetically arranged).
Recorded Index of Pedigrees in Deposited Collections.

Manuscript and Typescript Papers

D MSS. (Families): A collection of manuscripts classified under family name.

D MSS. (Places): A similar collection classified under place names.

Boyd's Marriage Index. This is in very many bound typescript volumes with entries collected from many printed and other sources available at the time it was prepared, and covering a period from 1500 to 1837. It is limited to certain counties, and they are not, of course, complete, as other sources have become available since its preparation. The counties covered are:

Cambridgeshire	Lancashire
Cornwall	Middlesex (including much
Cumberland (up to 1700	of London)
only)	Norfolk
Derbyshire	Northumberland
Devonshire	Shropshire
Durham	Somerset
Essex	Suffolk
Gloucestershire	Yorkshire

There is also a 'Miscellaneous' section including other counties. Surnames are arranged alphabetically, sometimes with male and female in separate volumes and sometimes with both combined in the same volume and alphabetical list. A key to this index is published (*see* Chapter Thirteen).

Apprentices of Great Britain. A typescript index to part of the register at the P.R.O. First series 1710-1762 with index of apprentice-masters. Second series 1763-1774.

Some London Burials 1583-1853 (16 volumes typescript).

Crisp's Apprenticeship Indentures (bound volumes of originals in two series, 1641-1749 and 1775-1888). There is a separate volume abstracting all in alphabetical order, the easiest means of reference.

Crisp's Bonds (bound volumes of originals, 1590-1847) indexed collectively in a separate volume.

Cuttings of births, marriages and deaths 1875-1894 and obituaries 1879-1894 from *The Times* and MS. yearly indexes of deaths only 1894-1931.

MS. list of those who paid tax on male servants in England and Wales, 1780 (from Treasury records at the P.R.O.).

Boyd's Citizens of London. Particulars of families largely 17th century) set out on printed forms with MS. index.

Boyd's Family Units. Similar to the last covering the whole country, but abandoned after 34 volumes.

Whitmore's MS. Notes (in binders)—mostly of London:

Aldermen	Arms	Funeral Certificates
Parishes	Pedigrees	
Wills	Pedigrees (Visitation)	

Bernau Index. Microfilms are available on application to the Librarian. This index contains many references to Chancery Proceedings, Court of Requests, Town Depositions and other documents at the P.R.O.

Trinity House Petitions. Applications of seamen and their families for pensions. Mostly early 19th Century.

Monumental Inscriptions and Brasses.

Williams Collection (relating to Welsh Pedigrees).

Smith Collection (extension of Visitation pedigrees and data on West Indian families).

Campling Collection (East Anglian pedigrees).

International Genealogical Index

Mention should be made of this important acquisition, previously known as the Computer File Index, together with the necessary microfiche readers. The microfiches (small sheets of microfilm which are magnified in the reading machine) which constitute the Index, contain many millions of names, mainly of birth/baptismal entries taken from parish registers and bishops' transcripts, or copies of both. The entries are arranged alphabetically under surname, with a separate series for each county. Coverage varies, London and Middlesex being the best. A search of the Index can prove very useful when there is doubt as to which parish to turn to next, especially in the Greater London area. Information obtained, however, should always be checked against the original. Copies of individual pages can be made on a Reader-Printer.

Owing to the popularity of this Index, it is necessary to telephone the Society in advance in order to reserve one of the reading machines.*

National Pedigree Index

This Index comprises slips on which anyone may place on record, free of charge, the existence of three or more generations in the male line. For a small fee, accompanied by s.a.e., others may apply for a search to be made in the Index for a particular surname in a given county. Further information can be obtained by writing to N.P.I. (with s.a.e.), c/o Society of Genealogists.

*For a full description of the Computer File Index see *The Genealogists' Magazine*, vol. 19, No. 5 (March 1978) pp. 162-163.

Chapter Nine

THE BRITISH LIBRARY, REFERENCE DIVISION

THE LIBRARY, housed at the British Museum,* is divided into two sections: printed books and manuscripts. Each is under a separate 'Keeper', as the heads of the Departments are called, and they in turn are under the British Library Board.

For access either to the Reading Room or the Students' Room of the MSS. Department passes are necessary. These are obtained by application in writing to the Library, specifying the particular purpose for which they are required, and supported by a recommendation from some-one of recognised position having personal knowledge of the applicant. Passes are usually issued for a period of 5 years, after which they must be renewed. For occasional use it is possible to have a day pass, but the same conditions must be fulfilled. Separate passes are required for the Reading Room and the Manuscript Students' Room. Full particulars can be obtained from the Library. A convenient way of obtaining such passes is to become a member of the National Art Collections Fund, the membership ticket of which carries with it the right to use the British Library Reading Room and Manuscript Students' Room and other libraries.

Among various leaflets available in the Reading Room *Notes for Readers* is a useful general guide, and Reader Guide No. 10 on printed sources for British family history

*Discussions are in progress as to the Library's removal to a new location.

and No. 8 on personal and family names are of particular interest to genealogists.

The libraries are closed on Sundays, Christmas Eve, Christmas Day, Boxing Day, New Year's Day, Good Friday and the first Monday in May; and also for the week following the last complete week in October. They are open on Easter Monday and on the Spring and Late Summer Holidays.

The Students' Room of the Department of MSS. is open on the same days as the Reading Room, but the hours are from 10 a.m. to 4.30 p.m. The annual closing is for the last complete week in October.

The main Reading Room, in which printed books are available, is a fine circular room some 140 feet in diameter lit from a dome, with a central space for the supervising officers, raised somewhat so that they can overlook the whole. Around the central space in a circular desk-height bookcase is ranged the General Catalogue in very many large volumes into which printed slips are pasted, evidently cut from a printed catalogue and its many supplements listing acquisition. On the desk top the volumes can be examined. Beyond this radiate the readers' desks with comfortable seats and local lighting. All round the outer wall rise tier upon tier of bookshelves filled with books. Nine tiers are accessible from the floor of the room, and readers can take out books from these without formality. Upper tiers above these are reached by galleries, but these, as well as the stock rooms outside the Reading Room, which accommodate the rest of the literally millions of books, are open only to the Library staff. When a book required has been found in the Catalogue, its reference or 'press mark' is filled in on a slip and handed in, when the book will be brought to the reader's seat within two or three hours. The shelves freely accessible each have their numbering clearly marked, so, if the press mark is found to be within the range of that numbering, no application need be made. It is useful to remember that slips for books can be post-dated and handed in or posted, so that the book will be ready to be collected at once on arrival on a future day. Also, books will be kept out at the end of the day for use next day, if this is asked for. Books may not be removed from the Library.

The North Library is used for those reading more valuable books, while the North Library Gallery provides for those wishing to see unbound parts of periodicals, large books etc. There is also a separate Official Publications Library for Government publications, and having on open shelves many of the standard volumes such as Acts of Parliament, Hansard, the main statistical books, etc. Except for those books to which there is free access, application-slips for State Papers completed with press marks from the General Catalogue are handed in at the desk or in the main Reading Room.

What is the particular value in visiting the British Library? It is the biggest library in the country, and, besides providing access to its valuable collection of early books, it is a complete reference library for all publications of the last century or more, except for books privately printed which may not always be found. The Crown had claimed on demand for the Royal Library a copy of any book which had been entered at Stationers' Hall, a right confirmed by statute in 1709,* and when this Library was presented by George II to the British Museum in 1757 the right was for a long time not seriously enforced. It was not till 1814† that the obligation was extended to cover all publications, and it was still only on demand, so many escaped. The Copyright Act of 1842‡ made automatic delivery compulsory, though it took a few years to enforce regularity. Since that time, at any rate, one library may have this book and another that, but the British Library should have them all.

*8 Anne, c. 21.   †54 Geo. III, c. 156.   ‡5 and 6 Vic., c. 45.

Perhaps if one considered the main items of general value to the genealogist one could include:

General genealogical reference books (which are kept together).

Society publications, such as those of the Harleian Society, British Record Society, etc.

Publications of the various local archaelogical or record societies, many of which touch on genealogy.

County histories.

Periodicals, such as *The Gentleman's Magazine, Notes and Queries, The Annual Register,* etc.

General directories and topographical books.

Many of the above may be referred to (possibly more easily) in other libraries. However, if there are particular books to which one is led by a clue but does not know where to find, it is these for which the British Library is most useful.

The national collection of newspapers is also of great value. These, except London newspapers prior to 1801, are kept in a separate repository at Colindale in North London, but, unfortunately, substantial loss was suffered from enemy action during the 1939-1945 war. If papers are found to be missing there, the publishers or their successors, if still existing, may have their own file and enquiry should be made of them.

The General Catalogue of the printed books has entries arranged alphabetically according to authors' names. Within each name, so far as practicable, the alphabetical order of initials or Christian names is adhered to. It is, therefore, important when noting an author's name for looking up his book to note the initials as well. Within the alphabetical order of authors are certain groupings, the most important for the genealogist being, perhaps, Eng-

land, London, Maps, Periodical Publications and News-
papers. 'England' is again sub-divided into such headings as
  Statutes.
  Parliamentary Papers.
  Departments of State (including County Councils and
    County Courts).
  Churches.
  Miscellaneous Sub-headings.

The 'Miscellaneous' section is of some importance, as it
includes National Societies, with an index of both sub-
headings and titles. 'London', too, has similar divisions
and the publications of such societies as the Harleian
Society, or the Historical Association will be found under
the 'Miscellaneous Institutions' section of 'London'. Both
'Newspapers' and 'Periodical Publications' sections have
their items arranged according to place of publication
with an index of titles.

At the end of each volume of the General Catalogue
there is another sequence on blue pages covering books
received 1971-75.

There is also a Current Catalogue on microfiche to be
consulted on microfiche-readers to the left of the Enquiry
Desk as one enters. This catalogue (at the time of writing)
contains all material dated 1976 or later and some dated
1971-1975. Also to the left of the Enquiry Desk is a small
card-index cabinet for certain books not yet entered in
the main catalogues.

When ordering books make sure they are not on the
open shelves (pressmarks 2000-2119) or at Woolwich. For
the latter consult the tables displayed in the Library: it
takes 24 hours or more to produce books from Woolwich.

It must be remembered that classification is by date of
acquisition which is not necessarily the same as date of
publication, because the Library is constantly acquiring
older books which were not previously held. Date of

publication will appear in each case against the book in the General or Current Catalogue.

The Genealogy section of books on the open shelves will be found in presses 2098-2101. They include the series of the Harleian Society and the Index Library (British Record Society) also that of the Scottish Record Society as well as Peerages, etc. County histories are in presses 2061-2068. In one of the bibliography racks (BB.O) at the inner end of the reading desks will be found the genealogical bibliographies, including Marshall's Guide and Whitmore's continuation of it.

The Department of Manuscripts is divided into Western and Oriental, the latter of which will not normally be of interest to the English genealogist. There are catalogues, many of them printed, of the various collections of MSS.— Harleian, Sloane, etc.—which are arranged according to the serial numbers of the MSS., but with alphabetical indexes to each volume. Those added since the original collections were acquired are classified as 'Additional MSS.' The printed catalogues are continued for recent additions in typescript in several loose-leaf volumes. There are similar catalogues of collections of Charters and of Additional Charters, and a printed index of place names referred to in the charters and rolls.

Besides these catalogues arranged serially there are a number of volumes forming a classified subject index to the MSS. There is a two-part general index containing a list of the subject classes followed by a limited alphabetical index giving details. The subjects most likely to interest genealogists are Biography, Topography and Heraldry with, perhaps, the State Letters or Private Letters. Subject index volume 51 (Biography—General) includes some parish registers and wills. Volumes 52-56 (Biography—Notes and Genealogies) refer to individual surnames arranged in alphabetical order.

There are card indexes of photographic negatives available, arranged according to the MS. number.

Amongst the MSS. of this Department will be found a large number of pedigrees, reference to which may have been found in some index or in Marshall's or Whitmore's Guides.* Many of them are probably of Visitation Pedigrees made at a time before these were generally available in printed form, though there are others the result of individual research. However, most of them will be found to lack specific evidence of the facts, so need substantiation before they can be regarded as proof.

As in the Reading Room, on a slip completed with the reference being handed in, the manuscript will be produced for the applicant.

There will also be found in this room a number of printed reference books which are useful in research, such as the *Dictionary of National Biography,* and some others, so that a move to the Reading Room to look up some point can be saved. There is a microprint copy of the complete Reading Room catalogue and there are also a number of catalogues of manuscripts of some other large Libraries. A walk round the shelves will give a good idea of what is available there.

Facilities are available for the supply of photoprints, photographs or microfilms: printed leaflets giving the terms with forms of application will be found in both the Reading Room and the MSS. Department's Students' Room. The 'electrostatic' process which is available for books is the cheapest, but the MSS. Department will not allow its use for old manuscripts, nor is it available for books published before 1800. The supply of prints may take several weeks or even months, but there is a 'rapid copy' service for electrostatic prints available to personal applicants only (not by post). This may only take two or three days.

*See Chapter Thirteen.

Whilst the British Library may be the greatest of the libraries, there are many others, both in London and in provincial towns, which can be of use to the genealogist. The searcher living away from London should not omit to investigate the possibilities.

Chapter Ten

OTHER LIBRARIES

OTHER LIBRARIES will vary considerably in size and scope. There are general libraries such as the London Library, the Bodleian at Oxford, or the Cambridge University Library, and local libraries in each city or borough, the larger of which, whilst having a special section of local books, approximate to a general library. There are also specialist libraries such as those of learned societies like the Society of Antiquaries, certain Government Departments with special spheres of administration or County Archivists or Record Officers who will concentrate on books relating to the particular county. Some will even have a general genealogical collection, as in Manchester, whose Public Library has published a catalogue of their genealogical books in three volumes. This is a very useful reference book, giving, for instance, a list of the parishes covered by the Phillimore series of printed parish registers in each county. County, city and borough reference libraries are free, but the libraries of societies are mostly restricted to their members, though facilities will usually be allowed to research students with or without payment of a fee.

Apart from the specific requirement of the Copyright Act for delivery of a copy of every publication to the British Museum, certain libraries have under various enactments been entitled to claim a copy. A clause in the Copyright Act of 1911 (unrepealed by the Act of 1956) requires delivery on request of a copy of every publication to the Bodleian Library, the Cambridge University Library, the National Libraries of Scotland and Wales, and the Library of Trinity College, Dublin. Such a request is, in fact, mostly made, and in any case publishers often send copies automatically without waiting for a request, so these libraries should have all British publications of value to genealogists, at any rate since 1911.

One must naturally adapt one's use of a library to the particular case in hand. It is no use looking at old numbers of *Landed Gentry* or *The Gentleman's Magazine* when dealing with a working man's family; on the other hand, a directory or a local newspaper might in such case be useful. One must investigate to see what can be found in a general library rather than expect to be told what to look for.

The genealogist should make a point of visiting public reference libraries in his neighbourhood. He may quite possibly find material which he can study more conveniently than by paying a visit to London. For instance, in one quite small provincial town is to be found a whole series of *Calendars of State Papers*: even a set of *Chronicles and Memorials of the Middle Ages* for anybody who wanted to study medieval history. Another has a number of volumes of indexes to the MSS. in the British Museum and some of the Reports of the Historical MSS. Commission.

An examination of the lending library section may provide something interesting. The reference for books on genealogy, following the decimal classification commonly used by libraries, is 929, so the relative books can be quickly found. Most reference libraries have a classified card index and the cards under the heading of Genealogy might be looked through, as some books may be out on loan and so not seen on the shelves. Whilst such searching in a public library will most likely not produce an answer to the immediate genealogical quest,

it widens one's knowledge of the possibilites and so in-
directly is a help.

Without a knowledge of the contents of all the main
libraries one cannot give any general guide, but one or
two categories might be mentioned.

A City or Borough Library

In any big Municipal Library will be found all the reference books of a general nature likely to be required, e.g.,
Dictionary of National Biography, atlases and gazeteers,
standard histories, etc. One item which may be useful is
the index to *The Times.* At Westminster City Library, for
instance, this is available back to 1855; at Guildhall in the
City of London it goes back to 1791.

This may be of little help to the genealogist in Manchester or Sheffield. He should make a point of investigating his own local libraries. He is certain to find something
of interest.

A public library, particularly that of a county town or
other large centre, is fairly certain to have a good collection of topographical literature on its own district. It
may be worth while paying a special visit to the library
of a district in which lived the family being traced. Not
only may there be books of local interest, perhaps privately
printed or otherwise rare, but there may sometimes be
manuscript records to be found.

Guildhall Library

Guildhall Library in the City of London deserves special
mention as one of the principal city libraries and with
some material of more than local interest.

Records here which should be specially mentioned are
those of the City Livery Companies with apprenticeship
and enrolment books, from which can often be found the
name and trade of the father. It is worth remembering that

before the 19th century all who practised a trade or craft within the City had to be 'freemen' of the City, which they could only become by membership of a Livery company.

The London diocesan records, including Archdeaconry and Commissary Court wills are deposited here. Other valuable material includes the list *London City Inhabitants 1695,* in part printed (London Record Society, vol. 2) and in part typescript in this Library. There is also a collection of London and provincial directories and poll books. A more recent acquisition is a copy of the I.G.I. ('Mormon microfiche'—see p. 70) covering the whole country.

The published *Guide to Genealogical Sources in the Guildhall Library* (1979) is a work of considerable interest to researchers, as is the fact that the Library remains open all day Saturday.

County Record Office Libraries

County Record Offices will have, in addition to their muniment rooms, a search room provided with reference books and works of local interest. Some now have copies of the International Genealogical Index.

Specialised Libraries

If one comes on some particular technical or otherwise specialised point one should have recourse to the library of the appropriate society. Many Government Departments have libraries covering their own field and these may be found of assistance.

Archives

It has been the practice of public authorities to preserve the various documents relating to the business of the authority, partly, no doubt, in case there should be any claim or dispute arising out of a public official's action. After some time had elapsed and this reason no longer held, they were often kept as a curiosity and, when their value was realized, for historical and antiquarian reasons. As a result, it will be found that with most public authorities there are preserved records of the proceedings of their controlling bodies and accounts of their financial officers, sometimes even with the vouchers for payments. Records of such transactions as the granting of licences, benefactions or endowments may be found as well as details of the general activities of the district, such as charitable and official functions. Much of this, if not strictly of genealogical value, may be of interest in extending information about known members of a family.

There are two directions in which to look for such information, viz. county and municipal authorities. Perhaps one might supplement these by a third semi-public type of authority, viz. any corporation or body which by endowment, subscription or subsidy carried on a public service, e.g. colleges and schools, hospitals and similar institutions.

The records of a county authority will be in the hands of the County Archivist, or, particularly in the case of more recent material, the Clerk to the County Council. One important category of records which may be found with such authority are the order books and other records of the Courts of Quarter Sessions for the county. These might be either of the full Court sitting four times a year or of the country magistrates who were empowered to make orders to a limited extent either individually or jointly with a fellow-magistrate. Besides a limited jurisdiction in criminal cases, the Quarter Sessions exercised a kind of supervision over local administration before the days of the County Councils, County Courts or the Local Government Board. Hence came before it

such matters as bastardy cases, breaches of apprenticeship indentures, disputes over parish settlement (*see* pages
39-40), all of which may yield genealogical information.

A variety of other documents will be found in the
charge of the County Archivist. Old documents relating to
a county tend to gravitate in time, when nobody wants to
keep them, to such an authority as the best centre for their
preservation (unless, relating to a particular borough,
they are sent to the borough authorities). Enquiry must
necessarily be made in the particular county, as the
documents available differ in each case. They may include
manorial rolls, parish registers, leases and other deeds,
manuscripts maps, etc.

A borough will be in possession of archives similar to
those of a county, but, being established as an administrative unit, often from quite early days, it will have, in
addition to records of its own Courts, the records of the
meetings of the various bodies which administered the
borough, the rolls of its freemen and accounts of its
financial officers. The borough may have supervised the
placing of apprentices in which case there may be apprenticeship records. Old charters and other ancient deeds
will be outside the scope of genealogy, at any rate for the
beginner. The extent to which old documents have been
preserved will vary, and enquiry must accordingly be made
in each case of the Town Clerk and Borough Librarian.

The Public Library in a large town may have a
separate Department of Archives holding collections
of the papers of local families as well as, possibly,
deposited parish records. Though one may not be searching for gentry, some member of such families as a magi-
strate or churchwarden may have retained or acquired a
collection of documents bearing on his duties. Recently in
Sheffield a long list of apprenticeships and a list of poor-
law papers have been prepared from such a source.

For both county and municipal collections there will
be some kind of index, again varying in extent and quality:
sometimes perhaps only a rough list, elsewhere a card
index, or even a published catalogue.

Of the semi-public authorities referred to above there
is a great variety: if a clue leads to such an authority,
investigation should be made. As has been mentioned,
in the case of the leading universities and schools there
are published records of their members. If one of the
family is known to have been a beneficiary of a charitable
institution, information about him and his family may be
found by enquiry of the authority concerned.

Chapter Eleven

ECCLESIASTICAL RECORDS

THE SUBJECT of parish registers and the bishop's transcripts, the best known of ecclesiastical records, has already been discussed in Chapter 4, as one can hardly touch genealogy without them. Other parochial records have been mentioned in Chapter 5. But there are a number of other sources of genealogical value amongst what might be called regional ecclesiastical archives.

The hierarchy of the established Church of England now consists of the two archbishops, the diocesan bishops with assistant or suffragan bishops, archdeacons, rural deans and parochial clergy. Except for rural deans, who do not seem to have any ancient records, and the assistant and suffragan bishops, each of these categories has archives representing the work of their predecessors. The archives of diocesan bishops were in the charge of their Diocesan Registrar and those of archdeacons were with their 'Official', usually a solicitor having a relation to the archdeacon like that of the Registrar to the bishop. In a different category is the Dean or Provost of a cathedral. He and the Canons who form the Chapter are responsible for the maintenance and services of the Cathedral and are not part of the episcopal administration authorities. The archives of the Dean and Chapter will normally be found in the Cathedral Library.

In recent years there has been a tendency towards transfer of episcopal and archdeacon's ancient records from the official custodian who is busy with current work to such a repository as a County or Municipal Record Office, where there is an expert staff for cataloguing and repair and proper storage accommodation, but some are still with Diocesan Registrars.

Marriage Licences

One of the most valuable items for the genealogist is the set of marriage licence 'allegations'. These are the documents on which the licences were issued and consist of an affidavit supported by a bond (the bond was discontinued in 1823*).

The affidavit is normally by one of the parties, often giving his trade or occupation, declaring that there is no lawful impediment by consanguinity or other cause. It may state the age of each party (valuable for tracing baptism record) or simply declare that they are over twenty-one. Where either of the parties is under 21, the consent of parent or guardian may be endorsed or be in a separate document, so giving valuable genealogical evidence. The affidavit will also state the Church in which the marriage is to be solemnized, a pointer to the parish register for the entry.

The bond is given by two sureties, one normally being one of the parties. It vouches that there is no impediment to the marriage. The bondsman's name is sometimes useful, being that of perhaps a father or brother.

The marriage licences issued were recorded in a book, sometimes reserved for them alone and sometimes containing probate records and other matter, and this may be found available. Original licences are not often found, as they were issued to the parties and have disappeared.

A large proportion of these marriage licence records have been printed, so reference should be made,

*4 Geo. IV, c. 76, section 15.

particularly to the Harleian Society and British Record Society series, though some ·have been printed by local societies or individuals.

Wills and Administrations

Though the ecclesiastical authorities should have handed over all testamentary papers to the Probate Registry when it was formed in 1858, many were apparently retained. This was in small part due to probate matter being in the same registers as the marriage licences just mentioned, but there was, for example, at Winchester a very substantial collection, probably remaining because the first Probate Registrar in 1858 was the Diocesan Registrar himself. Having both offices at that time in the same building, he no doubt did no moving about of the records and they were evidently moved away with the diocesan records when he left the building. The list of these, now with the County Archivist, has been published.*

Court Papers

The ecclesiastical courts, besides having jurisdiction over testamentary matters, heard many disputes about tithes, actions of defamation (slander), matrimonial disputes and sexual offences and various causes of a disciplinary nature arising from behaviour of churchwardens or other officials, disputes about seating, etc. Testamentary causes will, of course, quite often give information about relationships, but the others may not give much but biographical information, except for one important category.

As in the Court of Chancery, so in the ecclesiastical courts evidence was taken by deposition, and the deponent gave his place of birth, age, and previous places of

*Wills, Administrations and Inventories with the Winchester Diocesan Records. A. J. Willis (1968).

residence. The value of these records to the genealogist will depend very largely on whether they have been indexed. It should be mentioned that (as with most evidence of age) one must use the age given with allowance made for a margin both ways. Ages sometimes seem to be given to the nearest five years, and, no doubt, there were occasions when the deponent did not know with any accuracy.

There was one thing which, though nominally a matter for the bishop's court, was probably largely administrative in character, viz. the appointment of guardians for minors. This mostly arose when a minor on the death of his parents wanted to prove a will, but was not able to do so because of his status. The Court appointed somebody, usually a near relation, to act on his behalf. Two documents are found, the appointment of the guardian by name, signed and sealed by the minor (if under the age of seven, and so an 'infant', the deed was signed by a near relative on his behalf), and the Act of Court making the appointment signed by the Vicar General or his Surrogate. Sometimes several brothers and sisters are covered by the same deed. As the names and ages of the minors are given, as well as the names and parish of their parents and of the guardian (often with his relationship), these documents are of great value to genealogists (*see* Plate 2).

At Winchester all these Court papers are indexed in typescript, copies being available both at the Society of Genealogists' Library and at Winchester, so that any name can be turned up in a few minutes, but the same indexing may not be found in other dioceses. A calendar of these guardianship papers has been published.*

Winchester Guardianships after 1700, A. J. Willis (1967).

Clergy

Anyone interested in the clergy genealogically should not omit to look at the episcopal records, which include, of course, much about them. They will contain the administrative archives of ordination, licence to curacies, presentation and institution or collation to livings, nominations to perpetual curacies, non-residence licences, resignations and sequestrations. There may also be caveats against ordination. With the archdeacon's records should be induction mandates.

The most important of these for genealogists are the ordination papers, because these should contain a baptismal or birth certificate. Unfortunately this is sometimes missing, but, if not found with the papers for ordination as deacon, it may be with those for ordination as priest. Apparently both this certificate and testimonials were required on both occasions. The testimonial for deacon's orders will probably be from the College of the ordinand's University, signed by the Head and principal Fellows. It will give his degree and sometimes mention that he was a scholar or is a Fellow of the College. The testimonial for priests' orders is often signed by three neighbouring clergy.

Other records of ordination may be found in other places, but not with this detail. The Bishop's Register (a volume recording his official acts) lists the names at each ordination, usually with their degress and sometimes their College. There may be an ordination register extant for the period with the archives, and the earlier Visitation Books record the production of orders at the first visitation of a bishop after his consecration. These are often useful to show a move, as they mention date and ordaining bishop for both deacon's and priest's orders, the latter being often in a different diocese from the former.

The other papers referred to above will show movements of the clergy from curacy to curacy or living, and
again there may be registers giving this information as well.

The 'Subscription Books' should be mentioned, as these
contain the declarations of ordinands of adherence to the
Thirty-nine Articles and other requirements of Canon 36
of 1603 and of conformity to the Liturgy of the Church
of England. Similar declarations were required on institution to a benefice or licence to a curacy together with a
declaration against simony. The extent to which these
books have survived will vary in different dioceses, but
they are valuable for the signatures of the clergy.

Licences to Laymen*

The Church was interested in education long before the
State took notice of it and, no doubt, as the duties were
handed over to laymen the appointments were subject to
licence by the bishop. The Church, too, has long been
interested in the welfare of the body as well as the soul and
still is, as will be seen by their support of medical missions.
Physicians, surgeons and midwives were all licensed by the
bishop. These licences extend through the 18th century
and those for schoolmasters well into the nineteenth.

The value to the genealogist of this licensing is that
testimonials were submitted and these give information as
to where schoolmasters were teaching and to whom
physicians and surgeons were apprenticed (sometimes to
their father).

Parish clerks and sextons also were licensed by the
bishop and produced testimonials.

*See *Bishops' Licences to Laymen in the 18th and 19th
centuries.* Arthur J. Willis. *The Amateur Historian*, vol. 5 no. 1.

Records of Papists and Dissenters

Returns of papists from each parish may be found. Though sometimes these are only statistics, there may be lists of names.

Following the Toleration Act of 1688* dissenters were required to apply to the bishop of the diocese or the Sessions to have their meeting houses licensed. Applications will give name of owner or occupier of the premises and possibly have other supporters' signatures.

Discovery of the wanted name in either of these categories would turn the searcher to Roman Catholic records, such as those of the Catholic Record Society or to Nonconformist records, such as the non-parochial registers.†

Manorial Records

Bishops were in the past large landowners and if an ancestor was in a place found to be within an episcopal manor, the manorial records should be sought out. Manorial records generally are considered in the next Chapter (page 95).

Wherever the manorial records may be, there may be remaining in the Diocesan Registry or other repository something of the manorial papers or other deeds and records relating to land.

Tithe Maps and Apportionments

Following the Tithe Act of 1836‡ maps were prepared of all parishes and an apportionment made of the commuted tithe amongst the various properties. One copy of these may be with the parish records but there should be a set with the episcopal records. The sets of the

*1 W. & M., c. 18.
†See pages 35-36.
‡6 & 7 Wm. IV, c. 71.

Tithe Commission are at the Public Record Office. Each field or hereditament will be numbered and a list will give descriptions with names of owners and occupiers.

Other Records

There will certainly be other records which will vary from diocese to diocese, probably more of historical than genealogical interest. Such would be visitorship documents (arising from the bishop's position as Visitor to a College), replies from the parishes to Visitation Inquiries, consecration and faculty papers, surrogates' bonds, Registrars' accounts, general correspondence, etc.

Chapter Twelve

OTHER EVIDENCES

IN THIS CHAPTER something will be said of a variety of sources of information, some of which have been mentioned only incidentally in the previous chapters.

Manorial Records

There is a vast quantity of manorial records extant and scattered amongst most important repositories of archives in the country. A register is kept by the National Register of Archives, Quality House, Quality Court, Chancery Lane, London, W.C.2. Anybody interested in a particular manor should inquire of the Registrar there for information as to the whereabouts of such records. The *Victoria County History* which covers most counties has a section under each county dealing with manors and full reference to sources is given in footnotes.

The main items of interest to genealogists are the court rolls, the records of the courts held, usually with the Steward presiding. Important information is given by these, as they include admissions to tenancies on the death of a tenant. Normally the heir was admitted on payment of a fine and his relationship to the deceased is recorded. The Court also had a disciplinary function as is illustrated by the court roll reproduced in Plate 6, where it will be seen various tenants were 'presented' for not keeping their houses, hedges, etc., in repair.

Newspapers

The collection of newspapers in the British Library has been mentioned, but the searcher may find files in his local library or newspaper office. One must remember that in the earlier days of newspapers—the 18th and 19th century—facilities for delivery were not what they are today. There was no London paper delivered in the provinces on the day of issue. Local papers, therefore, contained the national as well as the local news, with the result that the latter was often limited to a few paragraphs about each principal town in the district. From quite early issues there are records of births, marriages and deaths, though, again, to a very much smaller extent than today. Local advertisements are sometimes of interest as containing particulars of properties, public announcements, etc.

Periodicals

A number of periodicals survive from the 18th century, such as *The Historical Register* or *The Gentleman's Magazine*, which recorded births, marriages and deaths and the movements of the nobility and gentry. Another periodical, *Notes and Queries*, which still exists today, sometimes refers to genealogical matter. There are usually index volumes to a series of this type of periodical.

There were at one time genealogical periodicals such as *The Ancestor, The Genealogist* or *The Pedigree Register*, and the indexes to these may be worth referring to. At the present day the main periodical on the subject is *The Genealogists' Magazine*, issued by the Society of Genealogists. This gives particulars of accessions to the Society's Library and records current matters of interest to the genealogist.

Poll Books

Poll books give a return of those who voted at Parliamentary elections and therefore give a fairly full list of the property owners of the district, the vote being then entirely based on property qualification. They are mostly of late 18th- and early 19th-century date, though a few of earlier date survive in some counties. Inquiry should be made of County Archivists who will probably know what copies exist. The collection at Guildhall Library in London has already been mentioned (page 83).

Monumental Inscriptions

This term (abbreviated by the genealogist to M.I.s) covers both gravestones in churchyards or inside churches and memorial tablets not at the place of burial. These sometimes give information as to dates of death, names of husband or wife, children, etc. Where the deceased had recently moved from another place, they sometimes give his former place of residence—or, if erected there, they give the place to which he had moved. The tracing of a family move is one of the constant problems in genealogical research. M.I.s mostly refer to the gentry, so one cannot expect to find memorials to the humbler families in the village church.

Churchyard memorials of the 18th century are often illegible now, though some of good stone in sheltered places can still be deciphered, if carefully examined, and others, the inscriptions of which have been re-cut, are reasonably clear. When the parish of the family is known, the churchyard should be visited with the possibility in view. For the earlier 19th century, before the establishment of the General Register Office, they make a useful supplement to information in the parish register, and even after that date they may amplify a death certificate.

There are records of M.I.s both in print and in manuscript. Inquiry should always be made at the church of the parish in question, as some interested local antiquarian society or individual may have deposited a record there, which would be kept with the parish documents. There is a collection at the Society of Genealogists and manuscript collections in the British Library and elsewhere and inquiry should be made at the local library in case there should be any there.

Biography

Many of the public schools have printed registers of their pupils, in some cases going back to the 15th century. The information given varies: sometimes it includes name and occupation of father. The Universities of Oxford and Cambridge have such printed lists, known as 'Alumni Oxon.' or 'Alumni Cantab.'. Some of the other Universities and each of the Inns of Courts have similar lists. Often a brief biographical note will be found in these registers.

Old Navy or Army Lists, Clerical or Medical Directories, etc., may be found useful and the more recently developed professions all have their archives. Where an official position was held there are lists of Sheriffs, Justices of the Peace, Mayors and Corporations, etc., which can be consulted.

If the individual has attained any fame or notoriety, he may appear in some national biographical volume. There are purely genealogical books, such as *Burke's Peerage* or *Burke's Landed Gentry* or general biographies such as the *Dictionary of National Biography* running into many volumes. For more recent times there is *Who Was Who*, reprinting from *Who's Who* of 1897 onwards the entries of those deceased. If a particular profession is known, there are, apart from registers of colleges and institutions already mentioned, such books as *British Authors before 1800* (H. W. Wilson, New York) or *Bryan's Dictionary of Painters and Engravers*. There are naval biographies— in fact most professions have made some effort in this direction.

Guilds and Trade Associations

Since the formation of guilds of merchants in early days there have been trade associations of various kinds. Such bodies as the various Livery Companies of the City of London, each of which relates to a trade, have records of their proceedings, admissions to their register, apprenticeships, etc. In the case of anybody in trade or business in or near London the records of the relative Livery Company should be looked up. They may be at Guildhall or still in the custody of the Company.

County or municipal authorities will probably be able to give information through their archivist or librarian of local associations which existed.

Family Histories and Pedigrees

A number of family histories have been prepared from time to time and these mostly include pedigrees. Some may be unreliable, particularly those which, to cover a gap in the evidence, say 'from whom was descended . . .'. It should be fairly easy to see whether each step is properly substantiated. Pedigrees will also be found in manuscript at the British Library and elsewhere. All these records again refer to the gentry and do not help the humbler families.

If there is any possibility that a right to armorial bearings has been recorded, the Visitation pedigrees should be examined. Many of these have been printed, but the original books are at the College of Arms. They were the result of tours by the Kings of Arms or their Heralds requiring claimants to arms to prove their title or renounce their right. They are classified by counties, and there are none later than 1668.

If a right to arms is to be established it will be necessary to prove direct male descent from one of the families whose arms were recorded at the Visitations, or from the holder of a specific grant and to register the pedigree with the College of Arms. Evidence must be supported by proof legally acceptable. A certificate will then be issued by the College that the right has been proved. The officers of the College of Arms, though appointed by the Crown, are mainly dependent on fees paid for the services they render: those who consult them must, therefore, expect to pay on a scale suitable for professional experts.

Leases

Leases may provide useful information about a family and its movements, though they are not often likely to give direct evidence of descent. Municipal or Church Authorities and any large corporation owning land are likely to have such documents amongst their archives.

Maps

Old maps are useful in identifying the hundreds or wapentakes into which a county was divided. A trace of a family may sometimes be found from a field or a copse with the family name (generally only on the larger scale maps). A map of the neighbourhood where a family lived should always be studied, as the configuration of the ground, directions of roads, etc., may provide a clue to movements. One must remember that transport was very restricted even as late as the beginning of the 19th century, and that a horse, with or without a cart, was the principal means of getting about for the ordinary person who had to travel more than walking distance.

Sundry Reference Books

Some of the most useful reference books are the various printed indexes to records. The Harleian Society and the British Record Society in particular have each issued a series of volumes including indexes to wills, marriage allegations and copies of parish registers. The catalogue of the British Library or of any library which has a series should be looked at to see whether there are any indexes referring to the county or diocese in which the searcher is interested. There are also officially published indexes to some of the Public Records.

Another group of books often referred to are books of topography, particularly the older ones which give information about old names of places, administrative boundaries, etc., at the time of their publication. It is often useful to know which 'hundred' or 'wapentake' a parish was in. Old histories will be found of each county, and a more modern production, *The Victoria County History*, covers most counties. For many counties the publication is in several volumes and in some cases the series is not yet complete. In the case of London *The Greater London Council Survey of London* may help to fill a gap.

Many counties have or have had archaeological societies which include genealogy among their interests, or even a more specialised Parish Register Society. These societies have usually published their transactions, as well as produced particular volumes on special subjects. There are also efforts of individuals who have written the history of a parish and included a copy of or extracts from the parish registers and other documents, or who have even made a survey of some particular branch of records over a wider field.

A most useful guide to what books are available is *A Genealogist's Bibliography* by C. R. Humphery-Smith (revised edition 1984).

Advertisement and Friendship

Help can sometimes be got by advertisements in a suitable periodical. The *Genealogists' Magazine* has a section for Readers' Queries, as well as space for advertisements proper.

I usually look through the Readers' Queries in the *Genealogists' Magazine* in case I can be of help, and one day an unusual name which I knew I had met caught my eye. I had been sorting and listing documents in the Diocesan Registry at Winchester and on looking up my index I found there was a stray will there under that name, deposited with the court in an ecclesiastical cause and never returned. This gave the inquirer two generations which he told me he had been trying to find for ten years.

Genealogists try, too, to help each other, knowing that if they have found something likely to be useful to another, the other searcher may never come across it and it will be lost to him for ever.

In this connection should be mentioned the growth of local Family History Societies and One-name Societies, which enable people of similar interests to meet and exchange information. They are run under the aegis of the Federation of Family History Societies which fosters many genealogical projects, including the ambitious scheme of compiling county marriage indexes as an extension of Boyd's work. Information as to these societies can be obtained from the local record office or reference library.

The Association of Genealogists and Record Agents

Those wishing to engage a professional genealogist are advised to consult the list published by the Association of Genealogists and Record Agents (A.G.R.A.) which gives names and special interests of members in various parts of the country. Copies may be seen in most reference libraries and record offices. The full list of members' specialisations and areas of work may be obtained from: The Hon. Sec., A.G.R.A., 31 Alexandra Grove, London N12 8HE, price 40p.

Chapter Thirteen

A BIBLIOGRAPHY FOR BEGINNERS

OUT OF the many books on the subject the following selection has been made with the beginner in mind. Those in print are obtainable by post or to personal callers from the Phillimore Bookshop, Shopwyke Hall, Chichester, Sussex PO20 6BQ. A general catalogue and sheets listing books on individual counties will be sent free on request.

TEXT BOOKS

A. J. Camp, *Tracing Your Ancestors* (1972)

A useful little book with some material supplemntary to that given here.

G. K. Hamilton-Edwards, *In Search of Ancestry* (revised edn., 1983)

General textbook with special chapters on naval, military and other professional records. Useful bibliography.

P. Spufford and A. J. Camp, *The Genealogists' Handbook* (Society of Genealogists, 1969)

A brief summary of the whole subject.

D. J. Steel, *Discovering Your Family History* (1980)

Linked to the television series on the history of the Honeycombe family.

C. M. Matthews, *Your Family History* (1982)

Advice on keeping notes and drawing up trees; guide to palaeography.

A. J. Camp, *Everyone has Roots* (1978)

An instructive guide, amusingly written by the Director of the Society of Genealogists.

Society of Genealogists' Leaflets:
No. 3, Family records and their
Layout (1977); No. 4, Note Taking
and Keeping for Genealogists (1977);
No. 7, the Relevance of Surnames
in Genealogy (1977); No. 9, Starting
Genealogy (1979)

INTERPRETATION

W. S. Buck, *Examples of Handwriting, 1550-1650* (Society of Genealogists, 1973)

Hilda Grieve, *Examples of English
Handwriting, 1150-1750* (Essex
County Record Office, reprinted
1978)

F. G. Emmison, *How to Read Local
Archives, 1550-1700* (Essex County
Record Office, 1978)

Photo reproductions of old handwriting in a variety of styles with
transcripts. Excellent for learning to
decipher old scripts.

C. T. Martin, *The Record Interpreter*
(reprinted 1982)

Lists of Latin and French abbreviations; glossary of Latin words; English
equivalents of Latin names.

R. E. Latham, *Revised Medieval
Latin Word-List* (1965)

Excellent for non-classical Latin as
used in English documents.

C. R. Cheney, *Handbook of Dates
for Students of English History*
(Royal Historical Society, 1970)

Invaluable aid for regnal years, saints'
days, legal chronology.

E. A. Gooder, *Latin for Local History*
(reprinted 1978)

To enable students to understand
deeds, court rolls etc. Illustrates
grammatical points and includes useful word-list.

L. C. Hector, *The Handwriting of
English Documents* (reprinted 1979)

Photographic illustrations with transcripts of mostly P.R.O. documents.
Useful introductory information.

PARTICULAR AREAS

G. K. Hamilton-Edwards, *In Search
of Scottish Ancestry* (reprinted 1983)

Scottish sources are often very different, so this is an invaluable guide.

A. Sandison, *Tracing Ancestors in Shetland* (1978)

F. Jones, 'An Approach to Welsh Genealogy' (*Transactions of the Honourable Society of Cymmrodorion*, 1949, pp. 303-468)

R. ffolliott, *A Simple Guide to Irish Genealogy* (Irish Genealogical Research Society, London, 1966)

D. Whyte, *Introducing Scottish Genealogical Research* (1982)

SPECIFIC SOURCES

Public Record Office, London. The following useful leaflets are available at the Public Record Office: No. 37, *Genealogy from the Public Records*; No. 2, *Census Returns*; No. 44, *Wills*; No. 34, *Death Duty Registers*; No. 26, *Apprenticeship Records*; No. 32, *Chancery Proceedings*; No. 9, *British Military Records as Sources of Biography and Genealogy*; No. 18, Admiralty Records as Sources of Biography and Genealogy

J. Cox and T. Padfield, *Tracing your Ancestors in the Public Record Office* (H.M.S.O., 1983)

Advice given on research to be done before a visit to the P.R.O., and sources available there, with a bibliography. New extended edition.

J. Gibson, ed., *Census Returns 1841, 1851, 1861, 1871 on Microfilm* (Gulliver Publishing Company and Federation of Family History Societies, 1981)

A directory of local holdings. This, and all other publications by J. Gibson, are available from the author, at Harts Cottage, Church Hanborough, Oxford, OX7 2AB

PARISH REGISTERS

C. R. Humphery-Smith, *The Phillimore Atlas and Index of Parish Register* (1984)

A valuable research aid illustrated with county maps (see next entry) and a full index of the whereabouts of all registers and transcripts.

also

Parish Maps of England and Wales and of *Scotland* (sold separately)

Show parish boundaries for each county and dates of earliest registers for every parish.

J. Gibson, *Bishops' Transcripts and Marriage Licences* (Gulliver Publishing Company and Federation of Family History Societies, 1981)

Use and whereabouts of these important sources.

Original Parish Registers in Record Offices and Libraries (Local Population Studies, Matlock, 1975, and supplements 1976, 1978, 1980)

Lists registers with their dates, and their present whereabouts, especially useful now that so many have been deposited in record offices and elsewhere.

National Index of Parish Registers (Society of Genealogists, 1974-1981) Volumes published include the following:
Vol. 1, General Sources before 1837; Vol. 2, Nonconformist Sources: Vol. 3, Roman Catholic and Jewish Genealogy; Vol. 4, Kent, Surrey and Sussex; Vol. 5, South West Midlands; Vol. 6, pt. 1, The North Midlands: Staffordshire, 1982; Vol. 11, pt. 1, Northumberland and Durham; Vol. 12, Sources for Scottish Genealogy and Family History.

Multi-volume series planned to cover the whole of the British Isles, with sections of general information and parish lists arranged by counties. Not all the volumes listed here are currently in print.

W. Leary, *My Ancestor was a Methodist* (Society of Genealogists, 1982)

Both this and the next book are useful for the specialised sources needed by those with Methodist or Jewish ancestry.

M. Gandy (ed.), *My Ancestor was Jewish* (Society of Genealogists, 1982)

My Ancestors were Quakers (Society of Genealogists, 1983)

N. H. Graham, *The Genealogist's Consolidated Guide to Parish and Nonconformist Registers, the Outer London Area* (1983); *The Inner London Area* (1983)

Handy paperbacks covering the confusing area of London registers.

Parish Register Copies (Society of Genealogists): Part 1, Society of Genealogists' Collection (1978); Part 2, Other Collections (1974)

Lists parish register copies held at the Society and elsewhere.

R. W. Massey, *A List of Parishes in Boyd's Marriage Index* (Society of Genealogists, 1974)

Registrar General, *Lists of Non-parochial Registers and Records in the Custody of the Registrar General* (H.M.S.O., 1859)

This volume may be seen at the P.R.O., Chancery Lane, where these records are now kept.

W. G. Tate, *The Parish Chest* (reprinted 1983)

Deals with parish documents often found with registers.

WILLS

A. J. Camp, *Wills and their Whereabouts* (1974)

Definitive guide to this complex subject with useful and comprehensive introduction.

J. Gibson, *Wills and Where to Find Them* (1974)

On similar lines to the above.

J. Gibson, *A Simplified Guide to Probate Jurisdiction* (Gulliver Publishing Company and Federation of Family History Societies, 1982)

Includes all the basic information needed by the genealogist in a small booklet. Available from the author (see under Public Record Office).

LOCAL RECORD OFFICES

J. Gibson and P. Peskett, *Record Offices and How to Find Them* (Gulliver Publishing Company and Federation of Family History Societies, 1981)

Routes to and location of local record offices, with advice for users.

Royal Commission on Historical Manuscripts, *Record Repositories in Great Britain* (H.M.S.O., 1979)

Corporation of London, *A Guide to Genealogical Sources in the Guildhall Library* (1979)

Description of manuscripts and printed books in this library famous for its genealogical collection covering other areas besides the London area which is its speciality.

C. C. Webb, *A Guide to Genealogical Sources in the Borthwick Institute of Historical Research* (University of York, 1981)

A valuable guide to source references in Yorkshire.

BIBLIOGRAPHY AND PRINTED PEDIGREES

C. Humphery-Smith, *A Genealogist's Bibliography* (1984)

Up-to-date replacement of Harrison's *Select Bibliography*.

G. Marshall, *The Genealogist's Guide* (Heraldry Today, 4th edn., 1974)

Exhaustive reference book of family histories in printed works.

J. B. Whitmore, *A Genealogist's Guide* (London, 1953)

Continuation of Marshall's *Guide*.

G. B. Barrow, *The Genealogist's Guide* (1977)

Compendious guide to printed works of family history.

T. R. Thomson, *A Catalogue of British Family Histories* (1980)

Burke's Family Index (Burke's Peerage, 1976)

A to Z key to pedigrees in Burke publications.

SOME REFERENCE BOOKS

L. W. L. Edwards, *Catalogue of Directories and Poll Books in the Possession of the Society of Genealogists* (Society of Genealogists, 1979)

P. H. Reaney, *A Dictionary of British Surnames* (1976)

A Topographical Dictionary of England and Wales, Scotland and Ireland (13 vols., 1840-1847)

Available in the P.R.O. and in some large libraries; useful for determining the Hundred in which a parish lies.

Road Atlas of Great Britain (Johnston and Bacon, 1977)

A small map-book, handy for carrying around, scale 3 miles to 1 inch, with index to 19,000 places.

Publications of:
The Harleian Society
The British Record Society
The Catholic Record Society
The Huguenot Society of London

A large number of volumes containing indexes and lists of wills, marriage licence allegations, transcripts of parish registers etc. Available in some libraries.

The Surtees Society

Covers the North of England only.

Victoria County Histories

Contain useful background information; footnotes can lead to other sources.

Guide to National and Provincial Directories of England and Wales (excluding London) before 1856 (Royal Historical Society, 1950)

Available in some libraries.

The London Directories 1677-1855 (Archer, 1932)

Chapter Fourteen

REGNAL YEARS

DATES IN OLDER MSS. are often expressed by the
regnal year. To be quite sure which year A.D. is referred
to it is necessary to know the day of the year on which
the reign officially began. For instance, the reign of
Queen Elizabeth I began on 17 November 1558. From
17 November 1558, to 16 November 1559, was therefore
the year 1 Eliz. The year 3 Eliz. would begin
two years later, i.e. 17 November 1560. The year 34 Eliz.
would begin 33 years later, i.e. on 17 November 1591.

There are in some cases short gaps between the official
dates at the beginning of a new reign, but, apart from these
and a complication in the reign of John,* a simple calcula-
tion from the opening dates given below will enable a
date expressed by regnal year to be identified.

Dates are not given here after the reign of Queen
Victoria, as the regnal year is then practically only used
for Acts of Parliament and in their case is expressed
differently, as it must be related to the Parliamentary
Session in which the Act is passed.

William I	25 Dec. 1066
William II	26 Sept. 1087
Henry I	5 Aug. 1100

*In the case of John, regnal years are calculated from Ascension
Day each year, which is a moveable feast in the calendar. For full
details see *The Oxford Companion to English Literature*, Appendix IV.

Stephen	26 Dec.	1135
Henry II	19 Dec.	1154
Richard I	3 Sept.	1189
John	27 May	1199*
Henry III	28 Oct.	1216
Edward I	20 Nov.	1272
Edward II	8 July	1307
Edward III	25 Jan.	1327
Richard II	22 June	1377
Henry IV	30 Sept.	1399
Henry V	21 Mar.	1413
Henry VI	1 Sept.	1422
Edward IV	4 Mar.	1461
Edward V	9 Apr.	1483
Richard III	26 June	1483
Henry VII	22 Aug.	1485
Henry VIII	22 Apr.	1509
Edward VI	28 Jan.	1547
Mary	6 July	1553
Philip and Mary	25 July	1554
Elizabeth I	17 Nov.	1558
James I	24 Mar.	1603
Charles I	27 Mar.	1625
Commonwealth†		
Charles II	30 Jan.	1649
James II	6 Feb.	1685

(Interregnum 12 Dec., 1688, to 12 Feb., 1689)

William III and Mary	13 Feb.	1689
William III	28 Dec.	1694

*See note on previous page.

†No regnal year was used during the Commonwealth 30 Jan., 1649, to 29 May, 1660. On the Restoration the years of the reign of Charles II were dated from the death of Charles I on the principle that he had been King *de jure* since then.

Anne	8 Mar. 1702
George I	1 Aug. 1714
George II	11 June 1727
George III	25 Oct. 1760
George IV	29 Jan. 1820
William IV	26 June 1830
Victoria	20 June 1837

The reader might like to be reminded here of the change in the method of dating which came into force in 1752 (see pp. 33 and 34).

It is also useful to know that early documents were dated by reference to the nearest festival of the church. *A Handbook of Dates* by C. R. Cheney gives all the saints' days and festivals. It also sets out all the regnal years with numbers referring to tables which provided calendars for each year.

Chapter Fifteen

SOME PROBLEMS SOLVED

*(Note.—The surnames in this chapter are fictitious,
but the incidents are based on fact.)*

1.—Charles East

Incorrect Age in Death Certificates Misleads

CHARLES EAST was an orphan who was brought up by
his maiden aunts Mary and Jane, now dead, his parents
John and Ann having died when he was quite young and
the actual year of the father's death not being known. A
search at St. Catherine's House gave his parents' marriage
and his father's death certificate, the latter including the
father's age at death. As is sometimes the case, the age
given proved to be wrong, so that the search for his birth
or baptism was prolonged and identity proved difficult.
Subsequently it was found that the father was born in 1838,
and not 1836 as was suggested by the death certificate.
The birth certificate was therefore available at St.
Catherine's House which it would not otherwise have been,
since general registration there did not begin till 1837. This
disclosed that Charles' father John was born in what was
then a small coastal town in Lancashire. Even with this
information identity was not easy, but eventually, with
the aid of one or two wills which mentioned three
children, John, Mary and Jane, his ancestry was established.

2.—James West

Value of an Unusual Christian Name

James West, a tavern house-keeper in Westminster, died in 1794 leaving a large family. His will disclosed, *inter alia*, that he had two brothers, Michael and Marmaduke, both farmers, the former in Buckinghamshire and the latter in Surrey. The natural inference that the family came from one of these areas proved to be without foundation. Marmaduke is not a common name, and as it was used in several subsequent generations it was suspected of being an ancestral name, perhaps for many generations. It was known to be a very popular name in Yorkshire. The calendars of wills proved at York were therefore consulted with the result that two of that name were found, one testator mentioning in his will sons named Michael, James and Marmaduke. An examination of the registers of this testator's parish gave all necessary particulars, including the marriages of two of the brothers: moreover, the actual date of baptism of the other was found to agree with that mentioned in the family papers of his branch of the family.

3.—Edward White

Family Surnames Given as Christian Names

Edward White died in 1825, aged 60, in a village on the borders of Oxfordshire and Berkshire, his origin being unknown. He was Lord of the Manor and had considerable property in the neighbourhood. A history of the parish, long out of print but subsequently located (being privately printed it was not in the B.L.), showed that the surname of the previous Lords of the Manor was Francis. As Edward White had given several of his children Francis as one of their Christian names, a relationship was suspected.

He also gave his children as Christian names other names which were evidently surnames—Hayward, Vince and Gatacre. On the wills of the Francis family being found and examined it was noticed that this family was related to Haywards, Vinces and Gatacres, farmers. One will showed that a member of the Francis family lived at a town in Northamptonshire, and in the parish registers there references were found to all these three families as far back as 1680. The marriage entry óf a White in 1760 in that parish described him as of another nearby town; this took the search there and gave the ancestry to Edward White. His relationship to the Francis family was found to be through the Haywards four generations earlier.

4. Thomas Mason

Unusual value from the records of a City Livery Company

Thomas Mason, whose ancestry was being sought, was known to have been a freeman of one of the City Livery Companies of London in the middle of the 19th century. Enquiry of the Company showed that he had been apprenticed to his grandfather, also a freeman of the same Company. A search of the books showed that two uncles, two cousins, two great-uncles and his great-grandfather had all been freemen too. In the record of the great-grandfather's apprenticeship was the name of his father. Though one might expect some information about a known member of a Company and, perhaps, the name of his father, it was a surprise to find such a complete pedigree available.

5. Joseph Yeoman

Flaw in an apparently perfect pedigree

The ancestry of Joesph Yeoman had been traced back through eight generations to an Essex farmer, George

Yeoman, with what seemed to be an undoubtedly correct pedigree.

However, during a search in a neighbouring parish for details of another branch of the family, a fault in the pedigree was found, quite by chance. A Thomas Yeoman, third from George in the direct line of the 'proved' pedigree, who had been named in his father's will to succeed to the family farm, had, in fact, died between the dates of his father's will and death, was buried in the neighbouring parish and could not, therefore, have succeeded. It was, however, known that a Thomas Yeoman did in fact succeed to the farm on the testator's death.

Following a long search it was found that the second Thomas was a distant cousin, who had succeeded not so much by virtue of kinship but because he had married a female descendant of an earlier generation, heiress on failure of the male line. It was from this second Thomas that Joseph was descended: George Yeoman was in fact a great-uncle of the second Thomas.

6. Flora Lambert (? Hutchins)

A Mistake in a Census Record

A census return gave a family listed thus with ages and places of birth:

John Lambert	Head
Mary Lambert	wife
Mary Lambert	U daughter
Robert Lambert	U son
Elizabeth Hutchins	M daughter
Mary Lambert	granddaughter
Flora Lambert	granddaughter

The two granddaughters are apparently daughters of a son of John Lambert, but there was no such son known of in the pedigree and hardly room for a place for him between his known brother and sisters. Suspicion was at once aroused that a mistake had been made and that Mary and Flora (both under seven years of age) were children of Elizabeth Hutchins. To solve the problem a birth certificate was searched for, Flora being chosen as having the less common name and both surnames Lambert and Hutchins being looked for in the index. Age and place being known, an entry of Flora Hutchins was easily found and on the full certificate being received it was seen that she was the daughter of Elizabeth Hutchins (*née* Lambert). The enumerator must have slipped in entering the surnames. This emphasises that even a written record must not be regarded as infallible.

7. Charlotte Anne's Marriage

The Value of Army Records

Charlotte Anne Browne was known to have married the following:

(1) in 1852 Charles Henry Osborne, who died 1854;
(2) date unknown, Richard James Wright, died 1859;
(3) in 1860, John Whitbread.

The problem was to find the record of her marriage to Richard James Wright. A search of the marriage indexes at St. Catherine's House revealed the marriage of a Richard James Wright in the December Quarter 1856, but Charlotte Anne Osborne did not appear in the index for the same quarter. However, the certificate was obtained, and proved to be the marriage of Richard James Wright to Charlotte Anne Maclean. No record of this marriage could be found, neither could any will be found for Maclean. However, as Charlotte Anne's husband Whitbread was a captain serving in India at the time of his marriage, a search was made of the *Army Lists* for the relevant period, and an Andrew Scott Maclean was found, also serving in India. A search of *Widow's Pensions Applications*

(WO 42) at the P.R.O. at Kew revealed that Charlotte Anne Osborne had married Andrew Scott Maclean in August 1854 in Ceylon, and that he had died in Bombay a month later.

8. Samuel Vachell Hicks

A Problem of Age

The 1875 marriage certificate of Samuel Vachell Hicks, bachelor, gave his age as 'of full age'. On the assumption that this implied over 21, a search of ten years was made, for a birth certificate for him but none was found. A subsequent search of his bride's address in the 1871 Census Returns revealed Samuel Vachell Hicks living there as a 'lodger', his age being given as 48, and his place of birth a parish in Devon. A search was then made of the relevant parish register, backwards and forwards from 1823, and his baptism was eventually found in 1817 (the unusual name confirmed that it was the right entry). But for the fact that he was living with his future father-in-law in 1871, it would have been very difficult to trace him. One might perhaps assume that he did not want his bride (who was 25 years younger) to know his real age, since when he married he was, in fact, 58!

9. Benjamin Palmer

Unusual Revelation of Illegitimacy

Benjamin Palmer, son of Henry Palmer and Sarah, *née* Hill, was believed to have been born in a parish in Oxfordshire in 1844, but no birth certificate could be found for him in that year. The 1851 Census Returns showed the household of Henry Palmer and his wife Sarah, and, living with them a child, Benjamin Palmer Hill, aged 6, 'son, illegitimate'. Another search was then made for the birth certificate for the date alleged, and he was found as the son of Sarah Hill. The marriage certificate of Henry Palmer and Sarah Hill showed that they were married five months after the birth of Benjamin.

Chapter Sixteen

CONCLUSION

THERE IS NO CONCLUSION to genealogy: it is an unfinished opera, the last Act of which is still in that ethereal pigeon-hole from which such compositions are drawn. Perhaps, however, I might summarise the possibilities in the diagrammatic form given in the Appendix on page 123, setting out the main themes of the Overture and the first and second Acts.

I have suggested in this diagram that a preliminary tree should first be drafted from family archives and personal inquiry, and that then an attempt should be made to take the line back beyond 1837 from four well-established sources. Of course, it does not follow that the line can for certain be traced back to 1837. There are many obstacles, such as the removal of a family from one place to another or a gap in the records, and it may then be necessary to test some of the possibilities suggested for the next stage. Once past 1837 so many official sources are lacking that almost anything *might* provide a clue. Skill lies in seeing possibilities, weighing them, picking out the probabilities with some idea of their relative likelihood, and testing them systematically and thoroughly.

The main problems for most of those who want to inquire into the genealogy of their family are distance from the sources to be investigated and/or lack of time. These can be met to a certain extent by carrying on the investigation by correspondence, but, naturally, this is not so satisfactory as direct searching. In some cases correspondence is no disadvantage, e.g., in obtaining certificates from the General Register Office, provided the data required are complete and the regulations and instructions of the authority concerned are strictly followed. On the other hand, for examination of a parish register one would be very much in the hands of the incumbent or parish clerk, who may or may not be skilled in reading the old handwriting and may or may not be interested.

Sometimes a half-and-half method may be found satisfactory, i.e., to pursue the subject oneself, using correspondence where practicable, but employing a searcher for special objects, such as examining a parish register for a particular purpose or for a given period, or examining the census returns of a stated parish for a stated name. The general direction of the search would be retained and the expert knowledge used for special purposes. One would, however, in this way lose the advice of the expert as to the general aspect of the problem and the likely sources to be tried.

There is, of course, the alternative of handing over the whole problem to the professional. This has the disadvantage that one is less in touch oneself with proceedings, so missing that interest which the hunt can give, and, of course, the cost is apt to mount up.

Speaking of cost, one must realise that there is absolutely no fixed relation between cost and results. One may spend a day going to see a parish register and the search may be in vain—it may even be that an entry that ought to be there is missing because there is a gap of some years in the record, an incumbent or parish clerk having been lazy. It is, therefore, quite impossible to answer such a question (which I have been asked) as 'How much will it cost to trace my great-grandfather?'

Hobbies cost money. Look at the photographer and what he spends on his apparatus and his running costs; the philatelist, sometimes forgetting that buying prices and selling prices are apt to be very different; or the antique collector, easily deceived unless he is an expert and often finding appreciation in value (if he could bring himself to sell) no more than, if as much as, that of cash invested in Savings Certificates. So the genealogist must expect expense—a certain amount of travelling, search fees in some quarters and time which might have been spent earning a living. If he has to employ agents or experts, this must mean more expense.

Perhaps one other essential should be emphasised. The search must be taken back systematically step by step. The tradition or wishful thinking of connection with some famous name 100 years ago must wait till the proof gets near that time. Otherwise one can fly off the track in many directions and be led into all sorts of by-ways and dead-ends, wasting both time and money. The by-pass round the great man will probably appear in due course!

One last word for the genealogist—PERSEVERANCE— though often it may be said of him

> *Vertentem sese frustra sectabere canthum*
> *Cum rota posterior curras et in axe secundo.*

> **Persius 5, 71**

Who like the hindmost chariot wheels are curst
Still to be near, but not to reach the first.

> *The Spectator*, No. 129

Mottoes of the Spectators, Tatlers and Guardians Translated
London 1737

SEARCH DIAGRAM

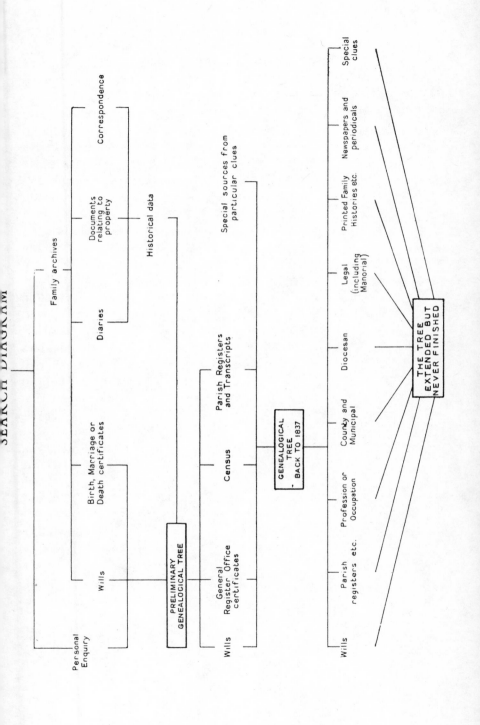

A GENEALOGICAL
ADVENTURE

by

Arthur J. Willis

James Willis son of Henry John and Mary Willis born at
Winchester 28th December 1839 married 7th May 1863 at
the Parish Church of West Hackney, Lond. Emma
eldest daughter of George and Jane Helmwood u. ..
born on the 20th day of June 1840 - Died 3rd Feb 1910 at
Buried on 7th February 1910 in the city of West... in Str... Hanwell Middx

Their children.

James Herbert Willis born at Barkly Road, Islington,
London on the 4th of March 1864. Baptized at the Church
of St Paul, Islington.

Emma Lilian Willis born at Southgate Road, Islington,
on the 12th of October 1865. Baptized at the Church of St
Peter, De Beauvoir Square, London.

Marian Helmwood Willis born at 116 De Beauvoir Road
in the Parish of West Hackney, London, on the 3rd of May
1867. Died 12th of July 1868 and buried in the Cemetery
Abney Park, London.

Emma wife of James Willis died on the 4th of May 1869 at No
116 De Beauvoir Road and was buried in the Cemetery at Abney
Park on the 7th of May 1869, The 6th anniversary of her
wedding day.

On the 14th of June 1873 the before mentioned James Willis married
at the Parish Church of Cheriton near Sandgate, Kent. Fanny
Leeson Griffiths daughter of George and Frances Griffiths of Long
Buckby, Northamptonshire, who was born on the 19th of January 1851.

Their children

A son, stillborn on the 5th of September 1874.

George Henry Willis, born at 12 Eton Villas, Belgrave
Road, Shepherds Bush, London, (now 41 Loftus Road) on the
21st of October 1875. Baptized on Christmas Day 1875 at
the Parish Church of Norwood, Middlesex.

John Burdett Willis, born at 41 Loftus Road, Shepherds
Bush, on the 6th of March 1877.

The foregoing entries made by me,
the before mentioned James Willis
this 19th day of March 1877.
J. Willis

John Burdett Willis baptized at the Church of St Stephen
Shepherd's Bush on the 10th of June 1877. JW

Plate 3. An Extract from a Family Bible.

Chapter Seventeen

INTRODUCTION

THE STORY opens with a boy of nine, sent home to boarding school by parents living abroad and spending a good deal of his holidays in the house of his grandfather in Ealing. Over the mantelpiece in the dining-room hung a low-relief portrait of an elderly gentleman modelled in wax and enclosed in a red plush mount and heavy rococo frame, with several miniatures below it. There was no instruction given, but it was vaguely understood that these were ancestors who had lived in Winchester. The shy boy did not like to ask questions, but he gathered that the family was in some sort of trade there.

Not long after this my grandfather died. The house remained in the occupation of his second wife and afterwards of their daughter, till some 40 years later on the latter's death it was emptied and sold. My father being in the 80s, the pictures mentioned above were passed to me, and the family documents with some oddments also reached me through him, unfortunately with evidence of censorship somewhere in their travels during the last 100 years.

An examination of what I received I found interesting. There were a few wills engrossed on parchment with the original probates attached and paper copies of others, a variety of small scraps of paper with genealogical notes and a record of gravestone inscriptions in Winchester, a seal with a head engraved which was evidently that of the wax portrait, a brass seal and a notepaper die each with the same heraldic crest. Amongst the documents were two in legal Latin puzzling to one with a distant knowledge of only classical Latin. There was a small devotional book published in 1714, and last, but by no means least, the family Bible, of large format, 4½ inches thick and of no inconsiderable weight.

Enquiry of my father elicited very little about the family history. He had no direct knowledge where the family had lived before they came to Winchester, only a rather vague idea that they came from Hertfordshire, settling somewhere in Hampshire, he thought Stockbridge, but he could not say with any certainty. He said the crest was that of the Hertfordshire family and that the family motto was *Non nobis, Domine.*

Chapter Eighteen

ARCHIVES AND HEIRLOOMS

MY FIRST THOUGHT was to put the material received into orderly form and to try to record the genealogical information available on one sheet of paper in the form of a family tree (*see* pages 190-196).

My grandfather, James of Ealing, and his two sisters, Sarah (Snow) and Emma (Jones) I had known personally, and I had some knowledge of their families. I supplemented this by enquiry from living members, and in the case of my grandfather's family I also had the family Bible. In this were recorded his own two marriages and the births, marriages and deaths (up to a point) of his children, and their issue (*see* Plate 3). I therefore had a fairly complete record of his family.

The next step was to examine the wills to see what earlier generations could be established from them. The backbone of any genealogical tree will be the male line. There were two male Willis wills, those of James (died 1858) whom I will call James of Winchester to distinguish him from James of Ealing, and John (died 1820). Each was on large parchment sheets with probate attached.

I had not received my grandfather's will with the papers, but I had been made aware of its contents some time before, as I was myself mentioned. Calling at Somerset House, it was turned up for me in a few minutes and, paying two or three shillings, I saw the record of this will in a large volume of typed record copies and arranged for a photostat copy to be sent me.

Of those wills which I had, I first looked at that of
James of Winchester. It was dated in 1854 and was rather
lengthy: in the opening lines the testator described himself
as a painter—the first piece of new information. He mentioned his son Henry John and his two daughters Emma
Bown and Maria. The will created a trust for the benefit
of the two daughters with remainder to the three grandchildren, children of his son Henry John. This established two more generations. The only bequest to his son
Henry John was the workshop, but a codicil dated six
months later revoked this and added the property to the
trust estate. What had Henry John done to deserve this?
Or was it that he gave up the family business and took up
something else, perhaps being given his portion in his
father's lifetime? Here was one puzzle asking to be solved.
At any rate I now had sufficient information to make a
complete pedigree back to James of Winchester, though
evidence on one or two details was still missing.

The next will to look at was that of John (died 1820).
He mentioned his wife Mary, son James, and daughter
Ann (Skeate) as well as his three grandchildren (children
of James mentioned above). He could be added in the
direct line and his daughter and her husband placed.

Amongst the documents was a half-sheet of notepaper
recording gravestone inscriptions in Cathedral Yard,
Winchester, in the hands of my grandfather and his second
wife. This gave the names of the wives of John and James
and a number of dates which could be filled into the
tree. It also mentioned John's son John who died in 1794
at the age of thirteen. This name was new and added
accordingly. This record of inscriptions gave a further
piece of information which might be useful, viz. that John
who died in 1820 was aged sixty-seven. His approximate
year of birth was therefore available.

At this John who was born about 1753 the family
record ended. There was no mention of anybody earlier.

The search must be pursued elsewhere. But where? For the moment this must wait whilst the remaining material is examined.

* * * * * * *

A copy of the will of an Ann Skeate dated 1825 was amongst the papers. It was a little puzzling. She mentioned her son-in-law, John Ralph Skeate, and his wife Ann, who was obviously the above-mentioned sister of James. It looked as if the testatrix, who also referred to James as her nephew, was John Ralph's mother, but the 'in-law' was a poser. She mentioned a string of married sisters, whose names conveyed nothing. I therefore put this will aside for the moment.

There was also a copy of a will of Ralph Skeate dated 1810 mentioning his wife Ann and his son John Ralph. Here evidently was the father-in-law of Ann Willis: he described himself as a carpenter. The will of Ann Skeate I had looked at was that of his widow. When I later discovered that 'son-in-law' was used in the past for 'stepson' the puzzle was solved. John Ralph was the son of Ralph by a former wife.

Before looking for earlier generations it seemed advisable to see what information there was in the remaining family documents, etc., about those persons already recorded in the pedigree.

A close inspection of the wax portrait mentioned above showed that it was inscribed by the artist 'Mr. Alderman Willis, Winton 1851' and signed by him, R. C. Lucas. James was therefore evidently an alderman of Winchester. The miniatures turned out from inscriptions on the backs to be two other portraits of him, one in 1806 and the other in 1823. The third was described as being of Hannah Bown, James's mother-in-law—unless her looks belie her I feel sorry for him!

A cutting from the *Hampshire Chronicle* of 1909, quoting an extract from '100 years ago', referred to the marriage of Ann Willis to Ralph Skeate of Sarum: it had a pencil note on it that she was the only sister of James Willis.

The wills of Mary Willis (second wife of John) and Emma Bown Willis gave no new genealogical information. They bequeathed some interesting personal articles, but the whereabouts of most of them is unknown to me.

One more will was available, that of Mary Gover dated 1845. She was mentioned in the list of gravestone inscriptions as a daughter of Benjamin and Hannah Bown, and was, therefore, a sister-in-law of James of Winchester. Apart from mention of her sister Sarah Willis and the appointment of James as an executor, her will was only concerned with her family, so added nothing.

A certificate of purchase of a grave in Abney Park Cemetery and a copy of the grave inscription there gave some further information about the first wife of James of Ealing, my grandmother, also of their child that died in infancy.

An old devotional book, *The Whole Duty of Man,* inscribed 'John Willis 1780', contained the birth entries of John (who died young) and James of Winchester, giving even the time of day of their births. There was one loose cover of a similar book containing the entries of James's three children.

There was a cutting from an agreement giving the signatures of James of Winchester and his son Henry John alongside legal seals. Somebody had evidently taken on himself the duty of censorship, destroying the rest of the agreement, but he wrote on it a date '1855'. The agreement between Henry John and his father (in the year after

the former was cut out of the latter's will) might have
been interesting, but its contents seemed gone for good.
There was one hope of defying the censor because on the
back of the cutting was written

It might be that the official filed copy could be found,
the word 'Bench' no doubt referring to the Court of the
Queen's Bench.

A small piece of paper evidently of 18th-century date
gave an extract from the will of one Nicholas Silver dated
1759 bequeathing certain property of his 'on the Middle
Brooks within the City of Winchester . . . now in the
several occupations of John Willis . . .'. This was interesting. Being amongst the family documents it probably
referred to a member of the family. It could not refer to
the John who died in 1820, as he would only have been
about six years old in 1759. It might be his father or,
perhaps, an uncle. There was no proof, but it might
fit into the jig-saw somehow, sometime.

There were two documents in Latin. One was on 18th-
century hand-made paper and evidently contemporary. It
was clearly dated as in the eighth year of Queen Anne
and referred to some transfer of property for which
somebody paid £200. There was mention of Winton

(Winchester) and four messuages and three gardens but no indication of their locality. The personal names were strange except for a good deal of repetition of Willus, Willi, Willo (which reminded one of learning Latin declensions). For the moment it must wait.

The second Latin document was equally puzzling. It was apparently a blank form referring to Parliament at Westminster in the reign of William IV. It was signed 'Grey' and sealed with a coat of arms, but none of the blanks were filled in. The signature was no doubt that of Lord Grey, Prime Minister of that time. It could not help genealogically so was left for later investigation.

Another scrap of paper in the handwriting of an uncle of mine noted that in *History of Winchester,* 1773, ii, 291, a John Willis is mentioned as having been elected a freeman of Winchester in 1730. This was too early to be John who died in 1820 but might well be a relation.

An exercise book with examples of coats of arms drawn and coloured by James of Winchester was in the hands of cousins who had received it through their mother, his eldest grandchild. A rough pencil sketch in it of the crest he used suggested that perhaps he found this whilst looking at some reference book in connection with his armorial studies.

There were several articles bearing this crest, viz. an old-fashioned pistol (with the crest and initials J.W. engraved on the butt), a brass seal, a notepaper die and my father's gold watch received from his father. There was no information about any right to arms, except the rather vague tradition which my father handed on that we were descended from a branch of the Hertfordshire family. There was no difficulty in looking up the arms, as a local Public Library had Berry's *Encyclopaedia Heraldica* and Fairbairn's *Book of Crests,* though both were apparently of early-middle 19th-century date. The first lists all family names alphabetically and gives the blazon of the arms (including the crest in most cases), the latter does the same for crests only which are also illustrated by a series of plates. The former quoted the crest as belonging to Willis of Fen Ditton, Cambridgeshire, and Horingsley and Bales, Hertfordshire. Neither of the two last places could I trace, even with the help of Bartholomew's *Survey Gazetteer of the British Isles* in the same Public Library, until some further light was thrown at a later stage showing that the names had been distorted, probably in copying from a manuscript without verification. It was, of course, quite possible that the alderman-painter, finding the arms as I had, fancied them for himself. However, the point was worth investigation.

A number of sundry other papers had no genealogical value.

Such was the collection that came into my hands. It was clear that there was no guide to earlier generations to be found there and that I must look elsewhere for myself.

Jonathon

To wit. **[W]** E *Wardens . . . .*
. . . .

Church-wardens and Overfeers of the Poor of the Parifh of *Eaft Woodhay* in the
. . . . County of *Southton* aforefaid, do hereby own and acknowledge
John Willis & Mary his wife & Mary & Sufana their Children
to be *our* Inhabitant*s* legally fettled
in the Parifh of *Eaft-Woodhay —*
aforefaid. **In Witnefs** whereof, we have hereunto fet our Hands and
Seals, this 27 Day of *January* in the *19* Year of the
Reign of our Sovereign Lord *George the Second* by the Grace of God,
of *Great-Britain, France* and *Ireland*, King, Defender of the Faith.
And in the Year of our Lord 174*5*.

Attefted by *William Annodft* } *Church*
John . . . . . . William Brand } *Warden*
the mark + of William Ecue

Robert Pile — } *Overfeers*
John Pile — } *of the poor*

To the Church-wardens and Overfeers of the Poor of the Parifh of
St Maurice . . . . . . of Winchefter
in the *City* of *Winchefter* or to any, or either
of them.

[W] E whofe Names are hereunto fubfcribed, two of his Majefty's
Juftices of the Peace for the *County* of *Southton* aforefaid,
do allow of the above-written Certificate. **And we do alfo**
certify, that *. . . . .*
the Witnefs who attefted the Execution of the faid Certificate, ha
made Oath before us that *he* did fee the Church-wardens and Overfeers, whofe Names and Seals are to the faid Certificate fubfcribed and
fet, feverally fign and feal the faid Certificate, and that the Name*s* of
the faid *. . . . .* whofe Names
are above-fubfcribed, as Witnefs*es* to the Execution of the faid Certificate, are of their own proper Hand-writing. **Dated** the *. . . .*
Day of *. . . . . .* in the Year of our Lord 174*5*.

**Plate 4. A Settlement Certificate (from the Parish Records of St
Maurice, Winchester).**
(Reproduced by courtesy of the Hampshire Record Office)

Chapter Nineteen

THE SEARCH BEGINS

HAVING TAKEN the necessary steps to get a reader's ticket for the British Museum Reading Room, I went on a visit of exploration. Venturing somewhat timidly to the central space*, I said I was interested in genealogy and mentioned parish registers. I was referred to several genealogical manuals in an open bookcase near by and recommended to look up the name 'Phillimore' in the General Catalogue, as he wrote a lot on genealogy. This advice started me off.

Amongst the manuals I found Marshall's *Genealogist's Guide* and under the name of Willis amongst references to other counties I found one to Berry's *Hampshire Genealogies* and another to Clutterbuck's *History of Hertfordshire*; these seemed the most likely in the list.

I found Clutterbuck's *Hertfordshire* in one of the accessible shelves, and taking it out looked up the reference I had found. There was a pedigree there of the Hertfordshire family of Willis (which I afterwards found was in some respects inaccurate) and I looked through it. This pedigree gave the family of a Richard Willis of Balls Park near Hertford, two of whose sons had been created baronets by Charles I, but showed that the baronetcies were extinct. There was a rather interesting connection with Hampshire in this pedigree. Richard of Balls Park had a brother Thomas of Ashe, Hampshire. It looked as if I was getting 'warm', for Ashe was a village only some 15

*There is now an enquiry desk just inside the Reading Room entrance.

miles from Winchester and a far cry from Hertford. There
was no mention of his having any descendants, but might
there be and could they have moved to Winchester?

The reference to Berry's *Hampshire Genealogies* was to
a family of Stoneham Park which, so far as I knew, had no
connection with ours, and which I verified later had a
different coat of arms from that of the Hertfordshire
family.

I also, as advised, looked up the name of Phillimore in
the index and found that he had published a number of
volumes giving copies of parish registers, including 14
volumes of Hampshire parishes. These were not on the
accessible shelves, but the Hampshire volumes were got
out for me. I first looked through the Winchester parishes
mentioned and noted the Willis entries. I found that in
almost all cases the record was of marriages only. However,
there was, apparently, at the church of St. Maurice,
Winchester, a marriage in 1743 of John Willis to Mary
Rummey. These seemed a possible father and mother of
John, who according to my information was born about
1753. The baptisms not being printed, it was evident that
an examination of the original registers of St. Maurice
must be the next step.

At the British Museum I also looked up the *History of
Winchester*, 1773, referred to in my uncle's note. I found
the reference which was to a list of 'the present freemen'
of the City. John Willis, elected in 1730, was third on the
list, being preceded by one elected in 1719 and one in
1729. He must, therefore, have been fairly old in 1773.
It might have been John who was married in 1743 or,
perhaps, his father.

It was clear that the British Museum had given me
enough information to go on with, and so I decided to
see what Winchester could produce. The registers of St.
Maurice were the first objective, and, calling on the
Rector, I arranged to see the registers. I looked first

for baptisms after 1743, the date of the marriage, and found those of a succession of daughters followed by that of a son John in 1753. This date corresponded with the 1820 burial record giving an age of 67, and it was, therefore, evident that John Willis who married Mary Rummey in 1743 was the father of John who died in 1820. I recorded the dates of the baptisms of all the children and looked for the burials of father and mother. I found a Mary Willis buried in 1758 and John in 1783. As some of the children were baptised after 1758 it looked as if John had married twice, the later children being those of another Mary (a very common name at the time). There was, however, no second burial, so I was left rather puzzled. A search backward in the registers of this church showed no earlier mention of the name, so it looked as if the family were not in the parish much before the marriage of 1743. I inspected the registers of St. Thomas, a neighbouring parish, but found nothing there.

John Willis and Mary Rummey and their children being added to the pedigree, the search began for the next earlier generation. I had noticed that the *Hampshire Chronicle* had been established in 1772, and, referring again to the British Museum, I found that there was no complete file there, though some numbers were recorded in the catalogue. However, a trip to the Newspaper Library at Colindale was in vain, as the files of this paper had been lost by bombing during the war. On enquiry, however, from the *Hampshire Chronicle* office in Winchester I found that they had a complete file there, so I paid another visit to the city. Unfortunately, there was no obituary notice in the paper of the 1783 death which might have given age, and so provided a valuable clue. The paper was then only a four-page newssheet, including, of course, the principal national news; local news was, therefore, very limited. Looking at one or two 19th-century issues at the time of the deaths of later members of the family, I found obituary notices, including that of the death of John in 1820; this gave his age and so confirmed the manuscript gravestone record which I had.

The problem of John who was married in 1743 remained. Where was he born and when?

Chapter Twenty

PROFESSIONAL HELP AND AN INTERVAL

AS I HAD LITTLE idea of where to turn and could afford little time myself, I thought it best to get professional advice and help. It seemed that in any case I ought to see whether there was any record of the arms at the College of Arms. I therefore wrote enquiring whether any family now used the arms which I had found given in Berry's *Encyclopaedia* and was advised that on payment of a fee a search would be made. I therefore called at the College and, leaving the pedigree so far as I had built it up, gave authority for the search. I was advised in due course that no member of my family had made any application and was given to understand that the arms were not recorded as now used by others. I was shown the Visitation Books of 1634 and 1684 in which the pedigrees were recorded by the Herald and signed by the member of the family giving the information. These showed the descendants of Thomas Willys of Horningsea, the grandfather of the two baronets but, of course, only showed those living at the time of the Visitation. I was told that the male line of the grandsons had died out, though there was a suggestion without evidence that the last member of the family, John, had refused the baronetcy because he was in trade and had gone North. There seemed no likelihood of descent from him and it appeared that for the right to arms I should have to look for connection with earlier generations.

Leaving aside the question of arms for the moment, I took professional advice as to what could be done to trace my line further back. It was suggested, and I agreed, that the registers of other Winchester parishes should be searched for the period 1700-1725 to see whether John who was married in 1743 was baptised in Winchester. At the same time I was told there were other important sources which should be examined, viz. the records of apprentices and wills.

I, therefore, now left the matter in professional hands, at the same time pursuing my own investigation when I was able to have a day or two free to do so. I tried not to interfere with the programme arranged for the professional genealogist, knowing that the amateur interfering in professional work is generally a nuisance.

I spent a little time at local Public Libraries to see what reference books there were which might bear on genealogy. There was, of course, the *Dictionary of National Biography,* but as far as I knew our family had never attained such distinction as would justify inclusion. However, it was interesting to see who with the family name was included and what they had done to deserve the honour. There were later reference books, such as *Who's Who* and *Who Was Who* (which keeps alive the *Who's Who* records which have been removed on death since 1897), but these were too late to be of use. I came across Burke's *Extinct and Dormant Baronetcies* which sets out the pedigree of the Willys family of Cambridge-shire. This was interesting but curiously silent about the John, grandson of the first baronet, not giving as one would expect the record of his death, only saying that his father Robert died in 1692 'leaving an only child John'. There was possibility for investigation here, though the baronetcy which he would have inherited if he had lived long enough was classified as extinct. It may be taken as fairly certain that full investigation was made at the time the baronetcy lapsed, but the vagueness did lend some colour to the story related by the College of Arms.

In another local Public Library I found some volumes entitled *Calendars of State Papers* referring to the 17th century. These contained précis of various official letters and State documents, the originals of which are preserved at the Public Record Office. The volumes were indexed and, as a matter of curiosity, I looked through the indexes for the name of Willis. I came across mention of Sir Richard and his activites in the Civil War, apparently not altogether faithful to the Royal family which had bestowed the baronetcy on him. Also there was a case of Thomas Willis of Ashe mentioned. He had been granted the office of Clerk of the Crown in Chancery by Charles I with reversion to his son Valentine. At the outbreak of the Civil War he had been deprived of his office and he petitions to be restored in 1655. In 1659 the claim is renewed by Valentine, his father Thomas being stated to have died in 1656, and the failure of his claim is recorded (on the ground that Charles I could not grant the reversion to one who was then an infant!).

On my next visit to the British Museum I looked up Ashe in a reference book I had seen (Marshall's *Parish Registers*) and found that a book had been written about the village, by one named Thoyts, which included the parish registers. I, therefore, had this produced and studied it. There was a record of the baptism of Thomas son of Thomas of Ashe, stating that birth and baptism had been at Wield. There was nothing to show the burial of Thomas (father or son) or the baptism of Valentine. However, the book produced an interesting clue. Amongst a number of historical references to the village was a quotation from *Royalist Composition Papers* (*see* page 59). Thomas of Ashe summoned in 1694 pleads that he has been robbed by the soldiery, is very poor, etc., and he mentions that his son Thomas died in March, 1643/4.

I knew now that Thomas of Ashe, senior, and his son Thomas were both dead by 1659 when a second son

Valentine was still living. There was no mention of any issue of either Thomas. Here I left the armigerous family for the moment.

I went through the 14 Hampshire volumes of Philli-more's *Parish Registers* again, making a note of all mention of the name Willis. I then had a fairly full record of Willis marriages in Hampshire in the 17th and 18th centuries, but, of course, some parishes were not repre-sented. I also came across the series of Harleian Society publications which included two volumes *Allegations for Marriage Licences granted by the Bishop of Winchester*. They are arranged with male names given alphabetically (with an index to female names) and give names of the parties, domicile, date and sometimes such particulars as sureties for bond or the phrase 'with the consent of his (her) father' (giving name), indicating that the man (or woman) was a minor. There were given in these volumes marriages of John of Hursley in 1718, John of Hyde Street, Winchester in 1711. Richard of Winchester in 1710 (marry-ing a wife from Andover) and another (Christian name not given) at Andover in 1716. These were all about the date to suit a father of John who married in 1743. But, of course, like most lists of old documents these records could not be relied on as being complete; moreover, marriages were not always by licence.

I asked my adviser to add Hursley to the list of parishes the registers of which were being examined. St. Bartholo-mew, Hyde (Winchester) he already had on his list, and I paid a visit to Andover myself. I found there the family of Richard Willis, apothecary, who was the Richard who was married in Winchester and whose second marriage was the 1716 marriage at Andover referred to above. He had several sons including a John baptized in August 1722. This John would have been 21 in 1743 so might have been the John married in that year.

About the same time I came across a reference in the Catholic Record Society and noted that the Catholic registers of Winchester were recorded in print by them. I found this volume available at the Catholic Library in Westminster and examined it for the period in question. Apart, however, from the marriage of an Ann Willis in 1738 there was nothing to help.

A visit to the Public Library at Winchester showed that they had in the Reference Department the set of Phillimore's *Hampshire Registers* and a good deal of local and topographical literature. There was also a book, *Hampshire Registers* by Fearon and Williams, which looked as if it might be useful, as it gave particulars of the periods for which registers were extant in each parish and information about other documents kept with the registers, the parishes being arranged alphabetically.

Looking again through the family papers I examined once more the will of Ann Skeate and noticed that the names of the sisters she mentioned corresponded with those of the children of John Willis who was married in 1743 which I had found in the parish register. It therefore seemed clear that this Ann, the wife of Ralph Skeate was Ann Willis (baptized 1747). She was, therefore, both aunt and step mother-in-law to Ann who married John Ralph Skeate!

Noverint Universi per præsentes; Nos John Willis de Hursley
in Com Southton Pipemaker, et Roger nipson
de Hursley Pipemaker teneri & firm —
Obligari Rev: in Christo Patri ac Dno Dno Jonathan
in D. Angl libris bonæ & legalis Monetæ Magnæ Britaniæ, solvend' ei-
dem Rev 7bi — aut suo certo Attornato, Executoribus, Admini-
stratoribus, vel assignatis suis: Ad quam quidem solutionem bene &
fideliter faciend Obligamus Nos & utrumque nostrum per se pro toto
& in solido, Hæredes, Executores, & Administratores nostros firmi-
ter per præsentes. Sigillis nostris Sigillat' Dat decimo septimo
dis Mensis May Anno Regni Dni nri Georgii
Dei gra Mag Brit Franc & Hibn Regis fidei
Defens & quarto Annoq Dni 1718°

THE Condition of this Obligation is such, That if there shall
not hereafter appear any Lawful Lett or Impediment, by Reason
of any Pre-contract, Consanguinity, Affinity, or any other just Cause
whatsoever; but that the above bounden John Willis a Batchelor
and Mary Marchant of Hursley aforesd Spinster

may lawfully Marry together, and that there is not any Suit depending
before any Judge Ecclesiastical or Civil, for, or concerning any such Pre-
contract: And that the Consent of the Parents, or others the Governours
of the said Parties, be thereunto first had and obtain'd. And that they
cause their said Marriage to be openly solemniz'd in the Face of the Parish Church of St Thomas in the City of Winchester
between the Hours of Eight and Twelve of the Clock in the Forenoon:
And do and shall save harmless, and keep Indemnified the above-nam'd
Lord Bishop his Chancelor and his Surrogates, and all other
his Officers, and Successors in Office, for and concerning the Premises;
That then this Obligation to be void and of none effect, or else to remain in full force and vertue.

Signat' Sigillat'n & Deliberat'
in præsentia.

John Willis
Roger Bond

Plate 5. A Marriage Allegation Bond (From the Records of the Diocesan
Registrar, Winchester).
(*Reproduced by courtesy of the Hampshire Record Office*)

Chapter Twenty-One

THE RESULT OF PROFESSIONAL SEARCHES

IN DUE COURSE I received a report of the activities of the genealogist employed. The search of all the parish registers in Winchester for the period 1700–1725 did not produce a baptism which might have been that of John who was married in 1743. There was a Willis family in the parish of St. John's in the Soke (the Soke being the part of the City east of the river and outside the old walls). There a John, son of John Willis, was baptized in 1707 but the register showed a burial of John in 1717, evidently the same. There was another family in St. Michael's parish with children of William Willis baptized between 1706 and 1712, but no John.

The registers of Hursley and Stockbridge (also King's Somborne adjoining) were searched, the former because of the marriage noted of John who was described as of Hursley, and the latter because of my father's vague idea that the family had once settled there. In neither case was there any mention of the name during the period.

The indexes to apprenticeship records had also been searched, but only three entries were to be found in Hampshire for the period:—

1715   John son of John Willis of East Woodhay to William Lawrence of the same, pipemaker.

1735   James son of John Willis of Kingswood to John Willis of the same, attorney.

1742   John son of John Willis to Henry Mathew, farrier of Henley, Hampshire.

These were rather disappointing as not showing any connection with a family in Winchester. Certainly Henley was not far from Ashe, where Thomas of the Cambridgeshire family had lived 100 years before.

A will which was looked for, though it might not throw any light on earlier generations, was the will of John who was buried in 1783. The indexes at the Winchester Registry were searched as well as those of the P.C.C. at Somerset House. However, no record of it was found. A list was made of all wills of the name of Willis at Winchester from the Civil War to 1800. In the case of one or two which seemed possibly to have some bearing the wills were examined and abstracts made. The will of John Willis of the Soke, proved in 1726, also one of John Willis, turnkey, proved in 1780 were seen. Neither was of any use.

The lists of Sarum wills, which happen to be in London, were also examined as the diocese of Salisbury was not far off, and if the family had lived over the Wiltshire border any wills would be in that diocese, not at Winchester. The lists provided no likely will.

In view of the information I had found about Valentine some search was made into published lists of members of the Inns of Court, Universities and of some of the principal old schools. Valentine was found to have been at Westminster School, Trinity College, Cambridge, and a member of the Inner Temple, being called to the Bar in 1653. There was no later information about him from this source.

As a family had been found in St. John's parish with the name of John, research into the registers of this parish was extended further. A baptism of John was found in 1672 and a marriage (probably of the same John) in 1694, but it was evident that there was no room for our John who married in 1743. He could not have been born after 1725 or he would have been under 18 at marriage and the chances of his being born before 1700 (i.e. being married over 43) were small.

The information found was all valuable, though apparently negative. There was no sign of our John in Winchester before his marriage in 1743, so it looked as though he was the first of his line in the city. Where did he come from? Why did he move? When?

Whilst in touch with the College of Arms, whom I had approached on the subject of arms, I took the opportunity to have translations made of the two documents in Latin. One proved to be a 'Foot of a Fine', the translation of which is given in the Appendix. 'Willus' I discovered was the Latin abbreviation for William and nothing to do with the surname Willis. There was no mention in this case of the name Willis, but the document did refer to premises in Winchester. It did not define the property clearly, but as the document was amongst family papers it seemed as if it had got detached from title deeds to family property, but there was at the moment no clue as to its connection.

The other Latin document was a blank form of proxy for use to appoint someone to act for the signatory in Parliament. It was signed and sealed by Earl Grey (the arms including supporters and motto agreeing with the recorded blazon), who evidently had not learned the danger of signing blank forms!

But by now costs of the professional investigation were mounting up. I was myself beginning to get some idea of the possible lines to follow and my interest in the search was deepening, so I decided I would carry on by myself in such time as I had to spare. I need not hurry, and if I found I could do nothing, I could always return to professional help.

As it happened, good luck was waiting only just round the corner.

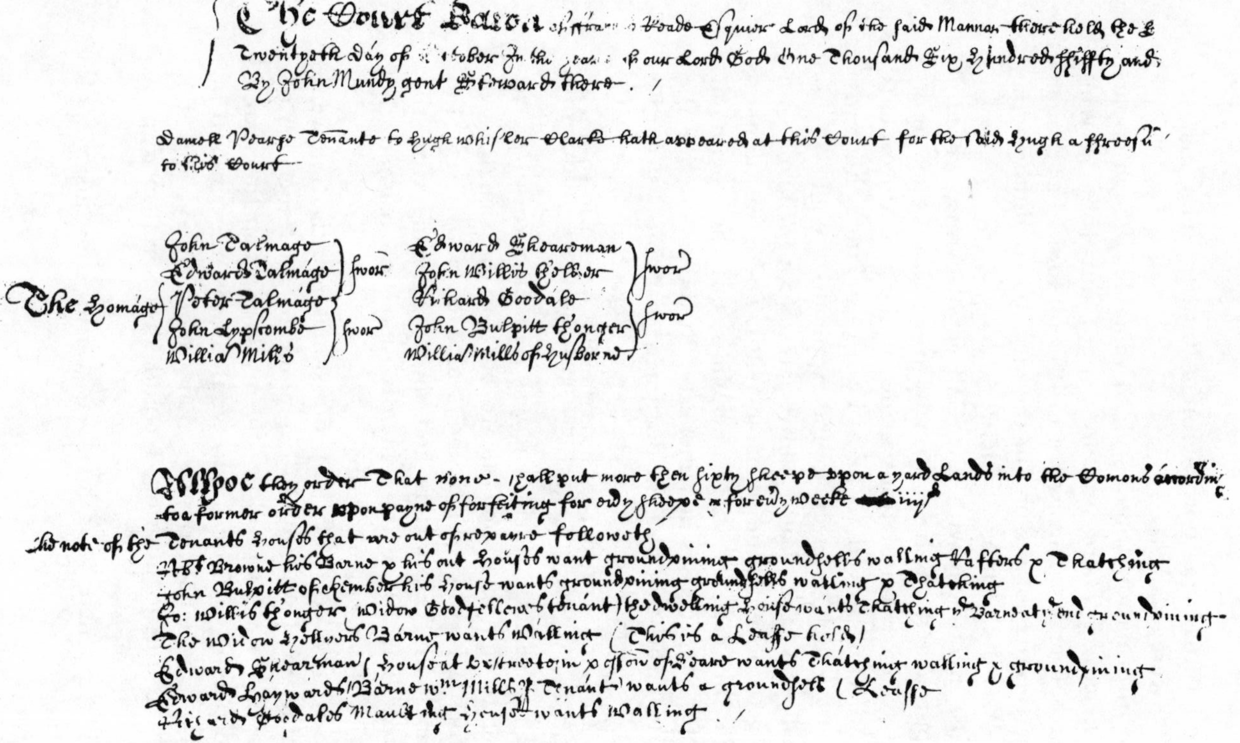

Plate 6. A Manorial Court Roll (from the British Library, Add. Charters 5077).

(By permission of the British Library)

Chapter Twenty-Two

EVIDENCE OF A MOVE AND EARLIER
GENERATIONS

I THOUGHT that the first thing to be done was to spread
the net a little wider in searching the Winchester parish
registers. I felt that one might go back to 1650 in all the
parishes to see who of the name was in Winchester,
whether any connection was evident or not. One might
by so doing find guidance where to look for the connection. At the same time burials might be examined up
to say 1775, as that of a possible father of John (married
1743) might be found. I had no time to deal with these,
so decided to employ a genealogist to work under my
direction instead of as before with more or less a free
hand. I therefore gave instructions for this extension of
the search over the wider period and for anything else
that could be done during the inside of a week spent in
Winchester.

The report of this extended search produced the piece
of evidence which was so badly needed. There were in
the church of St. Maurice other parish documents stored
in the vestry. These were turned out and amongst them
was found a book of settlement certificates.* One of
these was in respect of John Willis, his wife Mary and
two children (*see* Plate 4) and showed that their parish
of settlement was East Woodhay (in the north of Hampshire near the Berkshire border). In view of the
names of the children mentioned, there could be no

*See pages 39-40.

doubt as to identity, though I was puzzled at first that the date February 1745 was apparently before the second child was born. I had by then forgotten the change in the calendar in 1752*. Since, in fact, John was not sent back to East Woodhay, he evidently kept his head above water and did not become a charge on the parish.

'East Woodhay' rang a bell—in fact, the bell rang three times. There was in the apprenticeship records (*see* page 147) a John Willis of East Woodhay apprenticed to a pipe-maker in 1715, and I had also noted from the volume of *Hampshire Marriage Licence Allegations* (*see* page 144) a John Willis, pipemaker, marrying Mary Marchant, at St. Thomas, Winchester, in 1718, both described as of Hursley. Although either this John was older than usual when apprenticed or was married very young, there seemed little doubt that apprenticeship and marriage must refer to the same man. But why is he described as of Hursley? As the registers there had already been examined on the chance, I knew there was no record of the name there. It may, of course, have been the home of his wife, and he took what in these days might be called 'a suitcase qualification'. The third ring of the bell was a recollection that in my search of Phillimore's published registers I had found a marriage at East Woodhay in 1677 of John Wilis (*sic*) of Faccombe to Susannah White. If there were a son born to this 1677 marriage soon afterwards, he might have been married about 1698 or so and been father of John apprenticed in 1715.

The next step was obviously to search the registers of East Woodhay. I found by reference to Fearon and Williams' *Hampshire Registers* that the registers for East Woodhay for the period were still in existence. I therefore arranged for a genealogist to make a search of them for the period 1650-1750 (with burials to 1780) and had high hopes that they would provide evidence, possibly of

*See page 33.

more than one generation. However, except for one Willes in 1660 and the marriage already noted there was not a mention of the name. The register contained a list of seat-holders in 1698 but no Willis. This was a disappointment.

My thoughts then turned to adjoining parishes, as, though apprenticed in East Woodhay, John might have lived in or attended the church of another parish. I had noted in the printed marriages of Faccombe that the name occurred, but as far back as 1616.

On reference to *Hampshire Registers* I found that those of Ashmansworth had been lost by fire in 1810 and that those at Crux Easton did not begin before 1737 (with some births from 1702). Registers for the period were extant at Highclere and in some of the villages to the north and west of East Woodhay, but in view of the existence of a family earlier at Faccombe and a marriage licence recorded for Crux Easton I rather fancied that side of the parish.

'Pipemaker' . . . 'pipes'—what sort of pipes? It seemed most probable that the pipes were clay tobacco pipes. If so, they would be made where the raw material was available and some information might be obtained from the geology of the neighbourhood. Making enquiry of the Geological Survey as to whether there was any pipeclay at East Woodhay, Hursley or Winchester, I was advised that there was no record of any at the last two places, but that at East Woodhay at a point near to Hollington Brickworks there was a seam five feet thick, though the stratum is only usually found a few inches thick. Hollington Brickworks lay on the south-east side of the parish, under a mile from the boundaries of Faccombe and Ashmansworth and little more from Highclere and Crux Easton. It seemed fairly evident that this must have been the neighbourhood where the apprentice of 1715 worked.

The puzzle of the pipemaker being described in the marriage licence as 'of Hursley' still remained. If he was born about 1699–1700 he would have been only just over

[continued on p. 158]

Transcript of Plate Seven

In the Name of God Amen, I John Willis of Fackombe in the County of Southampton, yeoman, being of sound and perfect memory the Lord be praysed, doe make and ordayne this to be my last Will and Testament in manner and forme following vizt.: Imprimis I committ my soul into the hands of Almighty God my maker hopeing through the meritorious death and passion of Jesus Christ my Redeemer to receive eternal Salvation. And as for my body I committ to the Earth from whence it came to be decently buryed in Christian buryall after the discretion of my Executor hereafter named

> Item I give unto my daughter Anne the wife of George Penton one shilling
> Item I give unto my son John Willis one shilling
> Item I give unto my daughter Elizabeth the wife of Peter Jestis one shillinge
> Item I give unto my grandchild George Penton ten shillings
> Item I give unto my grandchild and godson Peter Jestis twenty shillings
> Item I give unto my grandchild John Willis ten shillings
> Item I give unto my grandchild Peter Willis five shillings
> Item all the rest of my goods and chattels and all other my substance

whatsoever which it hath pleased God to blesse me withall not before given or bequeathed I doe by this my present Will give and bequeath unto my trusty and well beloved son William Willis and make him sole executor of this my last Will and Testament he paying my debts and legacies. And I do by this my last Will and Testament renounce revoke and disannull all other and former wills by me made. In Witnesse whereof I have hereunto sett my hand and seale the sixth day of December in the one and thiryeth yeare of the raygne of the Sovereign Lord Charles the Second by the Grace of God Kinge of England Scottland france and Ireland defender of the fayth etc. annoque domini. 1679

Signed sealed and
delivered in the
psence of

Roger Cooke
Jasper Salter
William, Dowling
D
his marke

John Willis
W
his marke

Tertio die mens. Martii anno Dni (juxta &c.*) 1680 probatum fuit hmoi. (hujusmodi) testamentum in communi forma coram venli. (venerabili) viro Waltero Darrell S.T.P. (Sacrae Thelogiae Professori) Archino (Archidiacono) Archinatus Winton. Commissa adm(inistratio) executori in hmoi. testamento nominat(o) de bene etc. denique solvendo debita et legata etc. Jurato personaliter salvo Jure cuiuscunque.†

*Elsewhere found to represent 'juxta cursum et computacionem Ecclesie Anglicane'.

†On the third day of the month of March in the year of Our Lord 1680/1 the said will was proved in common form in the presence of the Venerable Walter Darell, D.D., Archdeacon of Winchester. Administration was granted to the executor named in the said will, he having personally sworn to administer justly and pay the debts and legacies etc. without prejudice to the rights of any other person.

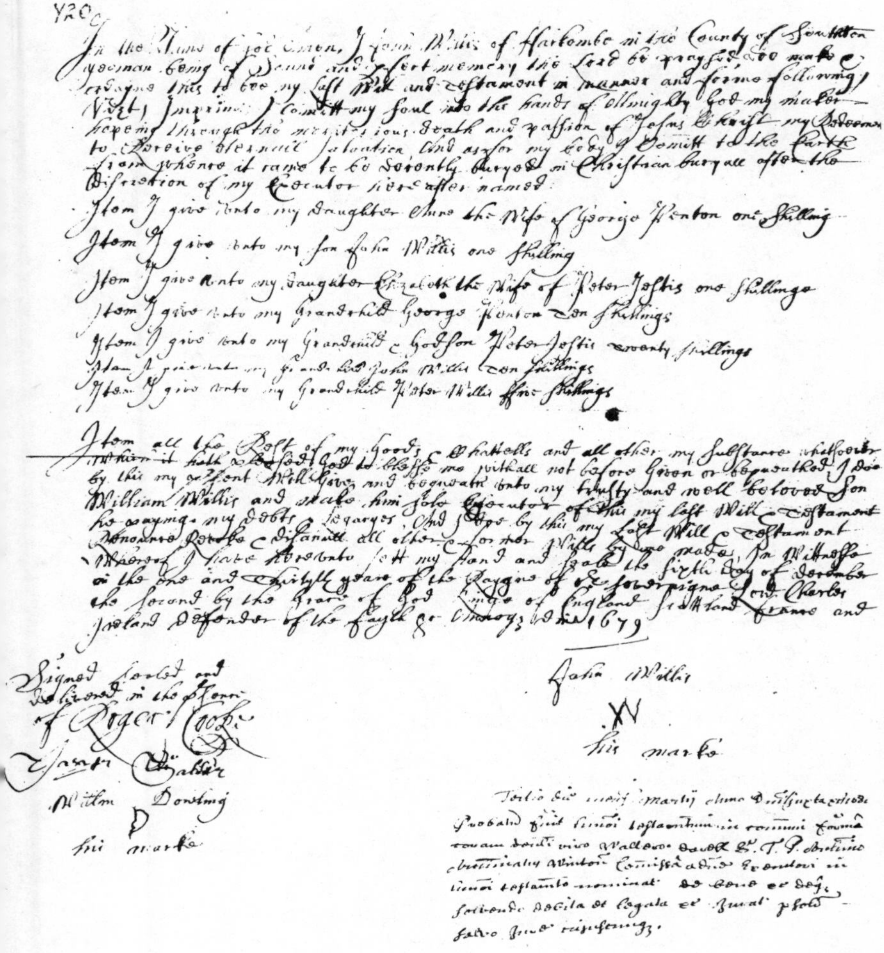

Plate 7. A 17th-Century Will (from the District Probate Registry, Winchester, Archdeacon's Court 1680).
(*Reproduced by courtesy of the Hampshire Record Office*)

[See transcript on facing page]

120 An Inventory of all & singuler of the goods Chattell & Catell of
John Willis the elder late of Hackcombe in the County of
Southton died seized of valued & prised the 29th
Day of Febervary Anno dom 1680 by yos whose names
are hereunto subscribed

Inprimis all his wearing Apparrell & money in purse
in the Chamber where he died ———————— 2 — —
Item one feather bede bedsteed & all
that thereunto belongeth ———————— 4 — 2 — 0 — 0
Item one Coffer one Chaire ———————— 0 — 4 — 0
Item certaine Cheese ———————— 0 — 10 — 0
Item in the Chamber over the hall
one flocke bede and bedsteed with all their
unto belonging ———————— 0 — 10 — 0
Item in the hall one peece of Andirons
three Cottrells one spit one fireshovell
& Tonges ———————— 0 — 8 — 0
Item one brasse pot one brass Keetle
alsoe one brase Candlesticke & foure
powter dishes one lantorne ———————— 0 — 6 — 0
Item one Joynett one forme
and two Chaires ———————— 0 — 6 — 0
Item foure flitches of bacon ———————— 2 — 0 — 0
Item one salt hire with out house
alsoe one Cheese press & little basckett ———————— 1 — 0 — 0
Item in the drinke house two barrills
one stand one table bord ———————— 0 — 10 — 0
Item in the Stable two horses &
the harness belonging to them ———————— 6 — 0 — 0
Item in the backside three Cowes &
three weaning bullocks
alsoe two steers pigs ———————— 10 — 0 — 0
Item one Carte ———————— 0 — 14 — 0
Item foure score sheepe ———————— 3 — 0 — 0
Item in the barnet certaine wheat ———————— 24 — 0 — 0
barly oats & pease threshed & unthreshed
Item Corne upon the ground being
by estimation eight acres of wheat & vetches ———————— 13 — 13 — 4
8 ———————— 0 — 0 — 0

Robert Sadler
Thomas Self apprisers
Sum totall 78 — 1 — 4

Transcript of Plate Eight

An Inventory of all and singular the goods chatle and catell late of John Willis the elder late of Fackoombe in the County of Southampton died seazed of valued and apprized the 28th day of February anno domi 1680 by us whose names are hereunto subscribed.

	li	s	d
Imprimis all his wearing apparill and money in purse in the chamber where he died	2	0	0
Item one feather beed & bedsteed & all that thereunto belongeth	2	0	0
Item one coffer one chaire		4	0
Item certaine cheese		10	0
Item in the chamber over the hall one Flocke beed & bedstead with all thereunto belonging		10	0
Item in the hall one peere [pair] of andiornes [andirons] three cottrils one speet one fireshoovell & tonges		8	0
Item one brase pott one brase keetle allso	1	0	0
one brase candlesticke & foure peuter dishes one lanterns		6	0
Item one joyend cubord one Forme and two chaires		6	0
Item foure fliches of baccon	2	0	0
Item one salt kiver in the outhouse allso one cheese preese and billet hatchets	1	0	0
Item in the drinke house two barrils one stand one table bord		10	0
Item in the stable two horses and the harness belonging to them	6	0	0
Item in the backside two cowes and three yearling bullocks	10	0	0
allso two store pigs		14	0
Item one carte	3	0	0
Item Fouer score sheep	24	0	0
Item in the barnes certaine wheat barly oats & pease threshed and unthreshed	15	13	4
Item come upon the ground being by estimation eight acres of wheat & vetches	8	0	0
Sum total	78	1	4

(sgd) Robert Lake
Thomas Self   Appreisers

[continued from p. 153] 18 on marriage, and the printed index of marriage licences usually said 'with the consent of his father A.B.' in the case of minors.

The registers of Faccombe and Highclere must obviously be searched. Highclere provided nothing at all, but at Faccombe there were several generations with relationships quite clear, the last John being baptized in 1678. He was the eldest of his family having several brothers and sisters and was evidently a son of the 1677 marriage referred to above. The registers, unfortunately, confirmed the gap from 1692-1700 in the marriages recorded (between the first and second volume). This was a piece of bad luck in a set of registers which from 1585 is fairly complete. There was not any sign of the baptism which would have been about 1699 or 1700, but it need not necessarily have been at Faccombe. It was quite common for a child, as happens now sometimes, to be baptized in its mother's parish, and that might be anywhere, though probably one of the surrounding villages. The registers of Combe, Linkenholt and several other villages around were searched for this baptism but without result. The most likely parishes were probably Ashmansworth or Crux Easton where the registers are wanting for this period. There being no other family in the surrounding villages it seemed reasonable to assume that the marriage was at Faccombe, Ashmansworth or Crux Easton and the baptism at one of the last two. Though there is no apparent break in the baptism record at Faccombe, it is certain that entries were sometimes forgotten, but one cannot claim an omission of that sort, failing evidence from some other source. In this case it seems just as likely that one of the other two parishes was the place of baptism.

An interesting piece of information comes from a list of seatholders of 1716 to be found in the Faccombe register. John Willis had two seats, one near the front on the north side, the other further back on the south side in the part reserved for women. The women or servants evidently sat apart. John Willis is described as of Cousin Street, no doubt the Curzon Street Farm now marked on the Ordnance map. It will be seen from the map that this is very near the Ashmansworth border and not far down the hill to Hollington Brickworks where his grandson was apprenticed the year before. It is not clear whether he is the tenant of Cousin Street as some rows behind him is 'Farmer Bunney of Cousin Street' and there is 'J. Talmage *for* Cousin Street'.

Some corroborative evidence to confirm the connection with Faccombe would be valuable. There were two possibilities, viz. the existence of a Bishop's transcript of the missing registers or the tracing of a will which mentions the family.

Enquiry of the Diocesan Registrar for the transcripts was, however, very disappointing. Except for one or two odd years of one or two odd parishes there was nothing before about 1780, although a book *Muniments of the Bishop of Winchester* (1912) refers to there being at that time parcels containing transcripts from 1663 to 1775. However, removal of some documents from the old Consistory Court to a muniment room at the Castle was still in progress and it was just possible that something might turn up. The matter was pursued to the Cathedral Library and to Wolvesey (the Bishop's Palace) but without result. The former had charge of archives of the Chapter (as distinct from the Bishop) and at the latter, though there were some manuscript records stored, there was no sign of the transcripts.

In the matter of wills I thought it advisable to see all the Willis wills at Winchester from the Civil War to 1800. I saw these and made short abstracts, but only one seemed as if it might have connection with the family. The will of John Willis of Faccombe made in December 1679 and proved in 1680/1 mentioned a son John and grandsons John and Peter. These relationships corresponded with the parish register record, Peter having been baptized in November 1679. The grandson of the will was evidently the John baptized in 1678 and the presumed father of the pipemaker. The will with the inventory that accompanied it is reproduced on Plates 7 and 8 and transcribed on pages 154 and 157. The will introduced a new fact that John the testator was a 'yeoman'. The inventory by its description of the contents gives an interesting picture of the homestead and throws light on the value of money in those days when 80 sheep were worth £24.

This will, however, did no more than confirm the record already made from the register. Failing a suitable will of someone with the family name there is always the possibility of a wife's father or uncle showing interest in the family. I had noted that John who married in 1677 married a White, and, moreover, she evidently came from East Woodhay, the marriage probably being, as is quite usual, in the bride's parish. I therefore searched the name White in the indexes of wills in the Winchester Registry. I found that East Woodhay was one of the Peculiars, and in the index to that group I found a will recorded of Walter White made in December 1711 and proved in 1713/4. This made son-in-law John Willis sole executor and the testator was evidently, therefore, the father of Susannah White married in 1677. It mentions his grandson John (the presumed father of the pipemaker) but says nothing about him. The interest of this will is the connection with East Woodhay and that his son-in-law is preferred above his own son as executor. The possibility suggests itself that the pipemaker's father was taken into his maternal grandfather's business at East Woodhay, whatever that may have been (unfortunately the testator does not state, as was commonly done, what his trade or occupation was); this would account for his leaving Faccombe for the adjoining village.

There was a further White will recorded in the index to the Peculiars as proved in 1731, that of a Walter White, probably the son of the first Walter White. Unfortunately the bundle to which it is referenced was missing, so what might have been a useful clue is lost.*

Another interesting point in connection with the will of Walter White proved in 1713 is that he mentions his daughter Ann Harding. In the register of St. Maurice, Winchester (the parish of our family), is an entry of burial of Ann Harding Willis in 1779. Did Ann Harding perhaps die a childless widow and leave money to the Willis family who named a daughter after her?

We are now in a position to put the circumstantial evidence to the jury as follows:

(1) A settlement certificate amongst the documents of St. Maurice, Winchester, shows John (m. 1743) as having come from East Woodhay.

(2) A John Willis is apprenticed to Wm. Lawrence, pipemaker of East Woodhay, in 1715. He would presumably be born about 1700 and just about the right age to be father of John (m. 1743).

(3) A John Willis described as pipemaker is married at St. Thomas, Winchester (described as of Hursley) in 1718.

(4) A John Willis is baptized at Faccombe in 1678, a date which would just fit for him to be married about 1698 and be father of the pipemaker apprenticed in 1715. There is a gap in marriages in the Faccombe registers 1692–1700.

(5) There is an unusually plentiful supply of pipeclay in the parish of East Woodhay at a point close to the borders of Faccombe, Ashmansworth and Crux Easton.

(6) John Willis (m. 1677), father of the last-mentioned John, was married at East Woodhay.

*This will has subsequently been found. Dated 5 Sep. 1728 and proved 22 Oct. 1731, it unfortunately does not help.

(7) The will of Walter White, father-in-law of John (m. 1677), shows that he was of East Woodhay.

(8) There is no record of any Willis at this period in the parish registers of:

East Woodhay	Hurstbourne Tarrant
West Woodhay	Vernham Dean
Highclere	Inkpen
Combe	Kintbury
Linkenholt	Enborne
Tangley	

Those of Ashmansworth and Crux Easton are wanting for the period. There is a burial of a John Willis at Hamstead Marshall in December 1715 which might be that of the pipemaker's father (soon after he had apprenticed his son), but there is nothing to explain why he should be buried there.

The verdict must be that John (bap. 1678) was married about 1698 and that his son John, born soon after, was the pipemaker, an apprentice in 1715, married in 1718, and father of John who was married in Winchester in 1743.

The answer to the Hursley puzzle and the short period between apprenticeship and marriage may have been that John broke his apprenticeship for a runaway marriage, was married under age without declaring it and gave a false address—there have been worse crimes!

The Faccombe family as appearing from the registers could be added to the tree. True, the marriage of John who was baptized in 1622 and died 1680/1 was not recorded, but this was evidently during the period of the Civil War. There is a gap in the marriages in the Faccombe register from 1646 to 1662. His first child was baptized in 1650.

There is one other loose thread in the pedigree of the Faccombe family. There is no record of the baptism of the first John, son of Richard. It would be quite natural for him to be baptized in the parish of his mother, or even, if Richard was the first member in Faccombe, in the parish from which his father came. There is no knowing where this may have been, but it may be found one day. The daughter, Rebecca, who died an infant, would, if she was a weakling, naturally be baptized in the parish in which her parents were living at the time.

This chapter will have given an example of how circumstantial evidence can be pieced together. Its acceptance does not mean that further evidence will not be looked for: though there may be no necessity to make the connection more certain, still it would give some satisfaction to come upon a Bishop's transcript of the missing registers or, perhaps, to find the will of the pipemaker or his father.

Whilst searching for this evidence I was at the same time on the look-out to see what detail I could fill in of the lives of those whose names I recorded. Whilst I proposed to pursue the line further if I could, it seemed an opportunity at this stage to take a breath and look round, marshal the information available and amplify it so far as possible. The three chapters following will give some account of my discoveries.

Chapter Twenty-Three

FILLING IN THE DETAIL—CIVIL RECORDS IN WINCHESTER

WHILST THE SEARCHES referred to in the last chapter were proceeding I took the opportunity of a few days in Winchester to explore the possibilities there. I did not expect to find anything that would extend the pedigree further, but rather was looking for fuller information on the generations already proved, particularly those who lived in Winchester. Two or three lines of approach occurred to me:

(1) There was a County Archivist at the Castle in Winchester and it was worth while enquiring what records were to be found there.

(2) the Town Clerk might have City records with some reference to the family.

(3) The Librarian at the Public Reference Library might be able to help.

(4) A systematic examination of the *Hampshire Chronicle* might produce some information: I had only searched for specific obituary notices.

(5) Although I had seen by then all the wills at the District Registry from 1660 to 1800, as the pedigree now reached before the time of the Civil War, earlier wills might be looked for. There was also the possibility of further 'in-laws' wills like that of Walter White which I had found.

The County Archivist I found had a good library of topographical and historical works on Hampshire and other books relating to the County. The object of my search being mentioned, the name Willis was looked out in a card index. However, the only product was one or two documents referring to the Andover family of the same name. The Archivist has charge of a very good series of Quarter Session records. They were, however, unindexed. I did not expect that my family would be amongst the delinquents, so just looked at one or two typical volumes to see what they contained. On a later visit it occurred to me that I might find John the pipe-maker summoned for breaking his apprenticeship or that John (married in 1743) might appear in a wrangle over his parish of settlement. I did later look at the relative periods in these records but could see nothing of this sort, though there were cases both on apprenticeships and settlement.

Several early poll books were in the County Archivist's library. The earliest is dated 1713 and mentions the family of John of the Soke. In 1779 and 1790 no Willis appears in Winchester but the poll book of 1806 includes John Willis.

From the Town Clerk I enquired about rolls of freemen of the City to see whether I could identify the John Willis who became a freeman in 1730. I was referred to the Public Library where certain rolls were kept, but they did not reach as far back as that. They did, however, show James as admitted a freeman on 9 October 1828, 'by gift', evidently an honour bestowed on him. After pursuing the enquiry again with the Town Clerk I ascertained that the freeman of 1730 was the son of Richard Willis, Bishop of Winchester. His son John left Winchester after his father's death in 1734. There is a large monument to Bishop Willis on the south side of the Nave of Winchester Cathedral, but so far as is known he was no relation.

The examination of the freemen's rolls existing at the Public Library led to an inspection of a variety of documents in the Muniment Room there. There was a large collection of City leases in process of being indexed. Having examined the card index over the principal period, I turned to the boxes of those still unindexed. Turning the leases over one by one I came across one or two relating to the family. One was a lease dated in 1789 to John Willis, victualler, of vacant ground 'whereon the Church of St. George sometime did stand'.

I was to find other evidence later to identify the victualler with John who died in 1820. The lease gave the dimensions of each frontage. On reference to old maps I found the location of St. George's Church at the corner of Upper Brook Street and St. George's Street and visiting it found a building existing which evidently dated from about 1800. There was built into it the remains of a stone wall—no doubt a relic of St. George's Church. The frontage dimensions corresponded with those on the lease, so this must have been the building John put up on the vacant site—no doubt for use in his painter's business. I photographed the building, and on a later visit found it in process of demolition. I walked over the ruins, but saw no Willis clues about.

Another lease was dated 1815 granting premises with a frontage on the north side of High Street to John Willis of the City of Salisbury. A further lease of 1829 granted what was evidently the same property to James Willis, painter, and this is renewed to James again 14 years later in 1843. Why was John described as of Salisbury? It is known that in 1809 when his daughter Ann married he was of Winchester. The possibility seems to be that he had retired and gone to live with or near his daughter who had married a Salisbury man. Perhaps he really took the lease for his son James. The 1843 lease specifies the size of the property (13ft. 2in. frontage to High Street and 72ft. 2 in. deep) and gives a plan. The adjoining properties are referred to by their owner's names so it has not been possible yet to identify the position.

A sidelight is thrown on rentals of the time. In the lease of 1789 the rental is 8d. a year and a couple of chickens for the Mayor (or 12d. in lieu of the chickens). In the 1815 lease rental was 12s. a year and the chickens as before, but the alternative to two chickens is now 2s. The leases of 1829 and 1843 continued the same rentals but added premiums of £38 and £45 respectively. There is even a manuscript 'Chicken Book' recording the payments to the Mayor in lieu of chickens.

In 1850 James jointly with a grocer, Edward Marmon, took a lease of the Fish and Poultry and Butchers' Markets for a year with the tolls for weighing cheese, etc., at the three annual fairs, for which they paid £91. Presumably they let out the sites of stalls at a profit.

At a later date when the connection with the pipemaker of East Woodhay had been established I was again turning over leases and my eye was caught by the name John Marchant taking a lease in 1745. Out of curiosity I opened it and found him described as 'pipemaker'. This was a coincidence, as John Willis the pipemaker had married a Mary Marchant. Reading further I found he was taking premises in 'Wongar Street', which was the old name for Middle Brook Street (the same street in which the family was known to be living in 1759 and the locality in which Mary Willis (*née* Marchant) was known to be living in 1757 (*see* page 172). It looks as though John the pipemaker married a sister of a fellow employee in the pipemaker's business of William Lawrence. Perhaps John Marchant was a bachelor or widower and came to live with or near his sister.

The Public Library Muniment Room provided much that was interesting and which it would take a long time to examine thoroughly. There was a Muster Roll of the

'Winchester Volunteers' showing James Willis enrolled in 1806, but mainly entered in lists of 'effectives entitled to exemption'—no doubt the 'reserved occupations' of the time! There were several books of mounted manuscript records and an array of newspaper cutting books. Amongst the former is the record of a special Council Meeting which decided to celebrate the christening of the Princess Royal in 1841 by holding a ball at which Mr. Willis was one of the stewards.

A Land Tax list for 1796–7 also appears amongst the mounted MSS. This must be a fairly complete list of house owners and occupiers. It shows Mr. Willis owning two properties, one in his own occupation, and it also shows Mrs. Willis (no doubt his mother, *née* Rummey) as an occupier of other property.

Amongst sundry MSS. in the Muniment Room was a series (incomplete) of lists of victuallers licensed in the City year by year. A list dated 1722 mentioned John Willis, painter-stainer, as surety for John Paul, licensee of the *Britannia*. The John who was born in 1753 would only be about 19, so could hardly be accepted as a surety. It looked, therefore, as though John who died in 1783 was a painter like his son (also a victualler), grandson and great-grandson. His son married a Mary Paul, no doubt the daughter of this publican for whom he was surety.

Another list of victuallers in 1782 showed John Willis as licensee of the *Cross Keys*, but there was no list between that year and 1793, in which year there was no mention of Willis. There was, however, a subscription list of innholders dated 1788 showing that John Willis subscribed five shillings to a collection for the Town Clerk for his help in petitions for removal of military quartered in the City (apparently in these days not of any benefit to the publicans). It is evident, therefore, that John gave up his licence between 1788 and 1793, and no doubt resumed his business of painting.

A list of constables over a period of years gave:

1782   Willis Jno., Junr.

This was John, licensee of the *Cross Keys*, taking his turn at the annual office.

Amongst the muniments were also some books in which the City Chamberlain's accounts and vouchers were mounted. There were a number of receipts for payments to Mary Willis for washing—evidently of the table linen after the civic banquets of the time. Some are signed by her, but others evidently only on her behalf. These receipts extend over a period from 7 October 1773 to December 1788, and may have referred to Mary (*née* Rummey) or Mary (*née* Paul) or each in turn.

An examination of *The Winchester Quarterly Record* 1848–69, on the Public Library shelves, revealed a number of references to James. On 22 January 1850 James was elected to the Committee of the Hampshire County Museum and on 12 August 1850, at a meeting of the Ancient Order of Foresters the Chairman was supported by him. On 10 November 1851 he was appointed (with others) to preside at Ward Elections, and on 9 October 1853 he was appointed a 'Commissioner for Taxes'. This periodical gave all the local day-to-day news, births, marriages and deaths, etc., for the short period for which it seems to have been published. Under date 9 November 1853 is an entry:

> The Council then proceeded to the election of three aldermen in the room of Messrs. Willis, Benny and Simonds whose term of office had expired. The voting papers having been received by the Mayor, the result was ascertained as follows: That Mr. Faithfull be alderman for St. Maurice Ward, Mr. Ventham for St. Thomas and Mr. Kelsey for St. John there were eleven votes. That Mr. Simonds be alderman for St. Maurice, Mr. Willis for St. Thomas and Mr. Benny for St. John there were ten votes. Messrs. Faithfull, Ventham and Kelsey were therefore declared duly elected. After a few observations of minor importance had been made, the Town Clerk said the next business . . .

James of Winchester evidently then made his bow to the
Council as alderman. What were the 'observations of
minor importance' one wonders? What did James mutter
into his beard?

Henry John appears under date 1 April 1850 as
appointed an Overseer for the parish of St. Thomas, and
in April 1852 he is appointed a Churchwarden of St.
Thomas. This appointment is renewed in 1853 but not in
1854 (the year of mystery). Finally, under date 19 August
1858 there is reference to James of Ealing:

> In his examination before the Civil Commissioners for a
> clerkship in the Office of Works, Whitehall Place, Mr. James
> Willis jun. late of this city was perfectly successful and duly
> obtained his appointment.

So, only a few weeks before the death of his grandfather,
my own grandfather is permanently established in London.

The Public Library has the only copy of an early directory of Hampshire dated 1784. This includes a list of
victuallers in Winchester and names John Willis as licensee
of the *Cross Keys* in Lower Brook. There is still a Cross
Keys Passage leading from Lower Brook Street into High
Street, but there is now no inn of the name. Gilmour's
Winchester Almanac and Post Office Directory of 1854,
also in that Library, mentions Willis & Son, High Street,
in the list of painters and refers to James Willis as Guber-
nator and Treasurer of Christ's Hospital (in Winchester)
and as a Director of Winchester Cemetery. A directory
of 1852 gives the address of Willis & Son as 84 High Street
and one of 1865 gives no Willis amongst painters but the
private address of 'Mr. Henry Willis' (James now being
dead) at Bar End and one of his two sisters at 2 Northgate
Villas. The latter, a house of about the Regency period,
has in recent years been demolished and replaced by a
modern shop block.

In examination of *The Hampshire Chronicle* one comes
across this sort of thing:

Mar. 6, 1837. 'Last evening a man in the employ of Mr. Willis, painter, was returning home with a load of turf with a horse and cart, the animal took fright when the man fell under the wheel and fractured his leg so severely as to render immediate amputation necessary.'

No Workmen's Compensation Act, still less a National Insurance Act! I hope James was generous.

Apr. 24, 1837. 'At the Annual General Meeting of the Mechanics Institute James Willis was elected to the Committee.'

A good deal of time could yet be spent in the Library Muniment Room or with the files of *The Hampshire Chronicle*, but it will be seen from the above that quite a lot of information has been gathered about the life of the family in Winchester.

Chapter Twenty-Four

FILLING IN THE DETAIL—PARISH
DOCUMENTS AND ECCLESIASTICAL RECORDS

THE DISCOVERY of the settlement certificates amongst the parish documents of St. Maurice, Winchester, suggested further investigation to see if anything else could be found there. Particularly there might be records of the interrogation leading up to the settlement certificate. A 'Book of Examinations' was found there which contained such detail, but, unfortunately, did not begin till 1781.

There was, however, a collection of old rate books (not a complete sequence) and they were examined for the name. The first mention appears in 1757 when in March and September are entered 'Widow Willis'. In 1759 the name does not appear. It looks therefore as if the burial at St. Maurice of Mary Willis in 1758 was this widow Willis, no doubt Mary (*née* Marchant) mother of John who was married in 1743.

The name appears again thus:

1770	19 Apl	Middle Brooks	Mr. Willis for late Earlys.
1772	19 Mar	Middle Brooks	John Willis.

In 1769-70 there had been entries under Middle Brooks of 'Mrs. Earle', and it seems that John Willis took over the property formerly occupied by her. In view of the will of Nicholas Silver leaving property in Middle Brooks occupied by John Willis to his nephew John Earle in 1759 (*see* page 133), it is probable that this same property came to John Willis in 1770 by purchase or perhaps under a will. This name of John Willis continues till 1783 when the entries are:

>4th Aug.   Middle Brooks Mr. Willis.
>19th Sept.   „   „   Mrs. Willice.

John was buried on August 3, 1783, and evidently his widow (*née* Rummey) continued in occupation.

From 1785 there are two entries on each date, both Mr. Willis and Mrs. Willis being mentioned. John the younger now had his own establishment and his mother kept hers. The name continues till 1805 when it disappears by May of that year. The family were later in St. Thomas's parish and this, no doubt, is when they moved.

The opportunity was taken to make a further search of the registers for the burial of Mary (*née* Rummey). There was no entry till 1810, which is known to be that of Mary (*née* Paul). No doubt, though the family had left the parish by 1810, she was buried where she and her family had lived for so long. A burial of Mary Willis, 7 July, 1791, was fairly certainly the infant child whose baptism as daughter of John Willis appears on 3 July 1791. There is no record of a child Mary surviving, as there most probably would have been had she done so.

The further examination of the parish registers of St. Maurice produced one or two of the name of Willis not known to be members of the family:

(1)   1779   Burial 13 Jan. Ann Harding Willis.
(2)   1780   Burial 2 Jan. Luke Willis.
(3)   1781   Burial 5 Oct. William Jourd Willis.
(4)   1782   Baptism 3 Nov. Peter son of Peter Willis.

Possible associations are as follows:

(1) The possible connection of Ann Harding Willis has already been mentioned (*see* page 161).

(2) Luke Willis of Ashmansworth of the Faccombe family who died in 1757 had a son Luke. The name is not common. Was this he?

(3) and (4) A Peter Willis married Susannah Jurd at St. Maurice, 21 May 1780, both aged 25. The burial of 1781 and baptism of 1782 were possibly of children of the marriage, though the baptism of the former does not appear. There is a Peter Willis of the family buried at Faccombe in 1757, but no record found of his family. He is described as of Uphusborne (i.e., Hurstbourne Tarrant), the registers of which do not throw any further light.

It looks, therefore, as if all four strangers may be connections of the family.

Though the marriage allegation of the pipemaker is recorded in a printed index,* I thought it would be worth while seeing the original record. This was turned up for me at the Diocesan Registry (*see* Plate 5). Besides giving John's signature, it provided the new information that the bondsman was a Roger Pond, also of Hursley and a pipemaker; this seemed to show that John did work in Hursley (pipeclay could, of course, be brought there, as no very large volume would be required), so it was worth while having seen the document. It will be noticed from it that the consent of parents is a condition, so one would not expect the consent to be expressed in the bond.

With the Diocesan Registry documents I found a series of Visitation Books, recording the names of clergy and churchwardens in each parish. Under dates 1686 and 1687 John Willis appears as churchwarden at Faccombe, also an earlier John in 1641 and 1642. Henry John was churchwarden of St. Thomas, Winchester, in 1851 and 1852, but not in 1853.

There was a tradition that James of Winchester had been responsible for painting the bosses of the Cathedral Choir ceiling, many with armorial bearings. I had noticed in the Press when these were recently repainted that they

Harleian Society, vol. 36.

had not been done for about 100 years. I made enquiry at the Cathedral Library as to whether any of the archives of the Dean and Chapter were there and found a Treasurer's Book 1846–60. This showed amongst expenses for repairs payment to Willis in 1851–54, the last including an item of £71 17s. 2d., a substantial sum, evidently for this painting. In 1855 the painting work was done by one Brown, who appears in a directory of 1859 as at 84 High Street. Evidently James retired from business in 1854 (the year of his will and of the codicil cutting out his son) and his son Henry did not carry on the business.

Once more the indexes of wills at Winchester were searched. The White will had been very useful and the possibility of other 'in-law' wills being of use must not be overlooked. To take the earliest: could any relative of Alice Hellier who married Richard in 1592 mention the family? Such a will might bring confirmation that John who married in 1616 was Richard's son, the baptism not yet being found. The list of Helliers was very long but there were none of Faccombe or Ashmansworth. Wills of some of Hurstbourne Tarrant and Andover were seen, but there was no mention of Willis; some wills, though in the index, were unfortunately missing. Then there was Rose Sherman who married in 1616, but the name of Sherman again drew a blank. Other names like Marchant, Harding, Jestis, were tried also without result.

Coming to a later date the will of John Paul of Winchester was found (he had been licensee of *The Britannia* and presumably the father-in-law of John of Winchester). This, dated 1797, was proved in 1807 in the Archdeacon's Court and left all his freehold messuages, etc., to John Willis of Winchester, painter-stainer, and the residue to the said John and Mary his wife, subject to some legacies to his daughter and grandchildren. This confirmed that John was again a painter by 1797 after giving up his licence of *The Cross Keys* (*see* page 170), and this will was evidently one of the sources from which the family obtained the property in Winchester which later they held.

Chapter Twenty-Five

FILLING IN THE DETAIL—LONDON

I HAD TO CONSIDER whether the vast amount of material in the many repositories in London was likely to be of any help in regard to an unimportant provincial family. In the case of the nobility and other prominent personages there are endless possibilities of finding correspondence or other documents relating to the family. There were, anyhow, one or two lines of approach which should not be overlooked.

Two Johns of Winchester being described as 'painter-stainers' it was worth enquiring what records of the City Company were in existence. An enquiry from the Company elicited the information that their records were at Guildhall. In the Guildhall Library I examined the rolls of members and apprentices of this Company, but found no mention of members of the family. The earlier John having been a pipemaker I looked in the same way for records of the Tobacco-pipe Makers' Company, but in their case there appear to be no records extant, except a copy of their charter.

At the P.R.O. information might be available if the family had been concerned in law cases. The examination of the Index to Chancery Proceedings and Feet of Fines is a long business but may be worth working through as occasion arises. The small portion examined so far has produced no information.

Further, curiosity will not be satisfied till an explanation of the lost deed (*see* page 133) is found. It was

apparently registered in the Queen's Bench, but the
Queen's Bench records for that period are not very good
and without the names of the parties in the case to which
it related this document is very difficult to trace. However, in time it may appear. It might be that Henry John
was involved in bankruptcy. The Index to *The Times*
for 1854 and 1855 was examined but the name does not
appear under the heading of Bankruptcies.

I also enquired at the P.R.O. about manorial records.
Quite possibly a 'yeoman', or substantial farmer, would
be a tenant of the local manor. I asked about the manors
of Faccombe, East Woodhay and Ashmansworth and was
advised that there were manorial rolls of Faccombe in the
British Museum and that there were at the P.R.O.,
amongst the records of the Eccleiastical Commission,
documents of the manors of East Woodhay and Ashmansworth.*

I found the Faccombe manor rolls in the MS. Department of the British Museum, but unfortunately they were
a very irregular series with many gaps. The roll of a Court
held on 20 October 1653† is illustrated in Plate 6 and
it will be seen that John Willis the elder is amongst those
sworn. At the foot (beginning with the line projecting into
the margin) will be seen:

> The note of the tenants' houses that are out of repayre followeth
> . . .
> . . .
> Jo: Willis th'onger (widow Goodfellow's tenant): the dwelling
> house wants thatching the barne at the end groundpining.

In two earlier rolls, of October 1592 and March
March 1592/3,‡ Richard Wyllys presents his excuses
through Thomas Hellyar. This is interesting as showing that

---

*These are now deposited at the County Record Office in Win-
chester.
†Add. Charters 5077.
‡Add. Charters 5070, 5072.

Richard who married at Faccombe in November 1592 was already of sufficient standing as a tenant of the manor to be one of the sworn jurors, and was not married in Faccombe simply because his bride lived there. Hellyar (or Hellier) was the name of his bride, so it looks as though she was of the same village, though Hellyar (in its varied spellings) is a very common name in the district; as I found when looking for Hellier wills which have a bearing.

I examined the list of manorial records of the Ecclesiastical Commission in the diocese of Winchester and found these to be very extensive. They were divided into groups, no doubt for administrative purposes, and one group seemed to consist of Ashmansworth, Woodhay and Ecchinswell, the last a village some way to the east on the other side of Highclere. Obtaining the necessary permission, I examined one or two records of likely date consisting of volumes of presentments, fines, etc. Examination of these is still in progress and, as a spare-time occupation, will take some time.

Though it was unlikely that any member of the family had achieved sufficient prominence to have any reference recorded in the manuscripts of the British Museum, I had found Calendars of Manuscripts and looked through their indexes for the name. There were a good many references to Browne Willis the antiquary. I also noticed some correspondence of Richard Willis of Andover, who beside being an apothecary was also apparently something of an antiquary. I had these documents out, mainly to see if there was any mention of his son John (baptized in 1722) as I was curious to know where he had gone. Though his son Thomas is mentioned in the correspondence, John is not.

In the British Museum Reading Room I found the Reports of the Royal Commission on Historical Manuscripts, some of which I had seen in a local Public Library.

These list in Appendices a very large number of documents in private possession, and I looked through them for the name of Willis. There was mention of several names I had met elsewhere: Thomas, Clerk of the Crown, Sir Richard and his alleged treachery, Simon secretary to Sir Robert Cecil, Browne Willis and others unidentified who might be anybody.

From a guide to National Directories* I found that there were some National Directories including Hampshire at the Guildhall Library in London. In one of 1823-4 James does not appear under the heading of 'Painters', but under the heading of 'Professors and Teachers' thus:

'Willis, James, (painting) High Street'.

As trade painters usually learnt by apprenticeship to a practising painter, one wonders what type of painting James taught. Had he aspirations for the art of scenic or portrait painting rather than the science of house painting?

In the Library of the Society of Genealogists is Pigot's *Directory for 1830* and in this James appears under the heading of 'painters' with an address 83 High Street.

A puzzle of fairly modern times still worried me. Henry John who apparently dissolved partnership with his father in 1854 was left out of his father's will. What was he doing till he died in 1867? His marriage had not been found and he seems to have left no will. I had the 1851 Census records of Winchester got out and found the census entry for his household. He was still, of course, a painter. His three children are entered as 'scholars' and their places of birth given. The eldest was born in Pimlico. Was that the clue to his place of marriage? It seemed quite probable. The map of London in Moule's *English Counties* showed Pimlico stretching over a larger area than we now know as Pimlico. It appeared to extend as far as St. Peter's, Eaton Square, which became a

*see Chapter Thirteen

separate parish church about 1830, so I enquired there for the marriage entry, but without result. Another possibility seemed to be the parish of St. John's, Smith Square, which I found now united with St. Stephen's—again a blank. Perhaps the marriage licences of London might give a guide. The indexes to records of these are at 1 The Sanctuary, Westminster,* and on searching the index to the Faculty Office licences for the two or three probable years the entry was found. The particulars obtained showed that his marriage was at St. James's, Westminster, and application to the rector produced a copy of the marriage certificate. If it were not for the clue given by the Census return, there would have been no reason to think that the marriage was in London.

*Marriage licences issued by the Faculty Office and the Vicar General are now at Lambeth Palace Library.

Chapter Twenty-Six

WHERE NEXT?

IT SEEMS CLEAR that the right to the armorial bearings, the examination of which was one of the reasons for my investigation, is a myth. The arms were probably assumed by James of Winchester, the flame of aldermanic pride being, perhaps, fanned by heraldic study undertaken in the course of trade. The Hampshire branch of the armigerous family have, in any case, been by-passed, though there may today be individuals who, all unknowingly, are entitled to the ancient arms, either as descendants of Valentine or of earlier generations than those shown on Chart 3. No title to the arms has yet been proved by anybody since the extinction of the two baronetcies.

As to the pedigree, having come to a full-stop with the marriage in 1592 at Faccombe, I looked around to see what prospect there was of finding anything earlier. I examined the calendar of early wills (before 1660) at Winchester and found two families at Ecchinswell, which is not far from Faccombe. Both wills were proved in 1570. One, of Nicholas Willes, mentions sons John and William, the other of Richard Wyllis mentions a son John. Both spellings are variants of the same name, so the two Johns in the same village make rather a complication. Neither will mentions any Richard who might be the Richard married at Faccombe in 1592. The latter will might be that of his grandfather, perhaps John being the father (whose name was carried on), but there is no evidence in the wills.

In view of the proximity of this family it was worth searching the registers of Kingsclere with which is Ecchinswell, a parish for a long time incorporated with Kingsclere. I accordingly arranged for a genealogist to make a search. The result was disappointing. There is a John Willis married in 1574/5, but this would be too late for a father of Richard, who was apparently established in Faccombe when he married there in 1592. There is a baptism of a Richard Welles in 1567 which might be of the Faccombe man, but as it is clear from other entries that there was a separate family named Welles, this is unlikely.

The Kingsclere register was examined at the same time for the baptism of John son of Richard of Faccombe, which, if there, might indicate that the move had been from Kingsclere, but there was no trace, though, unfortunately, some 30 lines in the period 1594–7 are illegible.

Looking at the records of registers in surrounding villages, I found that early registers were existing still at Hurstbourne Tarrant, and tried on the chance for the baptism of John in 1593-8, but without result. Richard might have come from some distant place and an unexpected clue might some day appear.

Turning over the card index one day at the Guildhall Library, I noticed a publication called *A Purveyance of the Royal Household* (1575) and that it referred to a number of villages, Faccombe, Ecchinswell, etc., with which I had by now become familiar. I had it looked out and found that it gave a list of those who contributed to the expense of a Royal Progress, probably most of the property owners in the neighbourhood. John Willis is mentioned twice at Ecchinswell—the references are such that they might be to the two Johns or to the same man. There was no Willis in the list at Faccombe.

The manorial records of Ecchinswell might produce some information. They are very extensive (*see* page 179), and it would take some time to go through them. As the family were tenants of the manor at Faccombe, the Chancery Proceedings at the P.R.O. are not so likely to help, but they are, of course, a possibility. The Willis wills at Winchester seem to be exhausted, though one may one day come across one of another name mentioning the family and giving a clue. In short, it looks rather as if, whilst keeping a look-out for possibilities, I must, like Mr. Micawber, wait for 'something to turn up'.

*   *   *   *   *   *   *

To show that things do turn up, a new clue appeared just as the first edition of this book was going to press. A genealogist friend, knowing of my problems, was searching for quite another purpose some records of the Weavers' Company in the library of the Society of Genealogists. He came across an apprenticeship of a John Willis to a Walter White dated 21 July 1712. White is, of course, quite a common name and Willis not uncommon, but the coincidence of the two was interesting, especially in view of the date. I had always been puzzled by the date of the pipemaker's apprenticeship (1715), when he would be about 15-16 years old, whereas apprenticeship usually began at 13-14.

If Walter White junior (*see* page 161) was a weaver in London, several things would be explained. It would be natural for him to take his nephew, John Willis, as an apprentice. The fact that the apprenticeship does not appear in the Inland Revenue records at the P.R.O. indicates that no premium was paid, which supports the idea of relationship. Moreover, Walter White senior would quite naturally make his son-in-law, John Willis, who was on the spot, his executor, instead of his own son. When Walter senior died in 1713/14, his son, the weaver, may have given up, left London and returned to East Woodhay, bringing his apprentice back with him and placing him locally with a pipemaker.

Knowing that many records of the City Companies were at Guildhall I looked up the guide to the City's records (*see* Chapter Thirteen) and found that there were deposited apprenticeship and freedom books of this Company, as well as Court minutes. There seemed, therefore, a good chance of identifying the Walter White or the John Willis in question. However, I was to be disappointed. Though I found the apprenticeship and freedom records of Walter White and confirmation of the apprenticeship of John Willis, there was no mention of locality from which they had come. I confirmed that John Willis did not take up the freedom at what should have been the end of his apprenticeship.

Whilst the verdict on the evidence must, perhaps, be 'not proven', it would only need a further slight clue to confirm the story.

All of which goes to show that a genealogist's motto should be 'Nil desperandum'.

POSTSCRIPT.—After reading the above the reader may think that a lot of unnecessary work was done. Why go to the British Library for books that are easily available at the Library of the Society of Genealogists, or the Public Library in Winchester? One must remember that there were at the time of this search (two or three years before publication of the book) no text books later than *How to Write the History of a Family* (Phillimore, 1887) and its *Supplement* (1900)! The searcher did not even know of the Society of Genealogists, and only at a late stage realised that there was such a thing as a County Record Office.

It will be realised that this search had an exceptionally good start because of possession of the 19th-century wills, which it might otherwise have taken time and trouble to trace. Others may not find a start so easy.

The 'Adventure' has been reprinted in its original form, as it is a factual account of what was done, and allowance must be made for the ignorance of the searcher. There have been changes in the location of records and even of names e.g., The British Library, but these have not been changed here.

P.P.S. Further research has revealed information on grandfather PAPAZOGLU. His Certificate of Naturalization at the P.R.O. (HO 1) dated 27 June 1861 shows him to have been a merchant of Manchester aged 33 and unmarried at that time. He and his father and mother were all born in Constantinople, although he maintained that he was Greek. His wife was English (*née* Bellamy).

Appendix

FOOT OF A FINE

Note: The bold type and italics are the author's in an attempt to make the reading easier.

This is the final concord made in the Court of the Lady Queen at Westminster on the octave of the Purification of Blessed Mary (*Feb.* 9) in the eighth year of the reign of Anne (*1710*) by God's grace queen of Great Britain, France and Ireland, Defender of the Faith, etc. after the Conquest, in the presence of Thomas Trevor, John Blencoe, Robert Tracy and Robert Dormer, justices and other faithful subjects of the Lady Queen then present there, **between** *David Clarke, John Lampard, John Broadwood* and *James Mitchell,* plaintiffs **and** *James Crosse,* gent. and *Elizabeth* his wife, *Robert Crosse, Joan Broadway,* widow, and *William Mumford* and *Brigit* his wife, deforciants; **concerning** four messuages and three gardens with appurtenances in the City of Winchester, **whence a plea of agreement** was summoned between them in the same court, namely that the aforesaid James Crosse & Elizabeth, Robert, Joan & Brigit recognise that the aforesaid tenements with appurtenances are the right of David, as those which the same David, John, John and James Mitchell have by gift of the aforesaid James Crosse & Elizabeth, Robert, Joan, and William & Brigit, and they remitted and quit-claimed them from themselves, James Crosse & Elizabeth, Robert, Joan & William & Brigit & their heirs to the aforesaid David, John, John & James Mitchell & the heirs of David for ever. **And furthermore** the same *James Crosse & Elizabeth* granted for themselves and the heirs of that James that they guarantee to the aforesaid David, John, John & James Mitchell & David's heirs the aforesaid tenements with appurtenances against the aforesaid James Crosse and Elizabeth and James' heirs for ever. **And further** the same *Robert* granted for himself and his heirs that they guarantee to the aforesaid David, John, John and James Mitchell & David's heirs the aforesaid tenements with appurtenances against the aforesaid Robert and his heirs for ever. **And in addition** the same *Joan* granted for herself and her heirs that they guarantee to the aforesaid David, John, John and James Mitchell & David's heirs the aforesaid tenements with appurtenances against the aforesaid Joan and her heirs for ever. **And also** the same *William & Brigit* granted for themselves and William's heirs that they guarantee to the aforesaid David, John,

John & James Mitchell & David's heirs the aforesaid tenements with appurtenances against the aforesaid William & Brigit and William's heirs for ever. **And for this** recognition, remission, quit-claim, guarantee, fine & concord the said David, John, John & James Mitchell gave the aforesaid James Crosse & Elizabeth, Robert, Joan & William *two hundred pounds sterling.*

Public Record Office Ref. CP 25 (2)/964, 8 Anne, Hilary.
Translated from the Latin by the College of Arms.

THE FAMILY OF

WILLIS

OF FACCOMBE AND WINCHESTER, HANTS., AND EALING, MIDDLESEX

Notes:

Richard Wyllys appears in the Court Roll of Faccombe Manor, 22nd October, 1592, and 22nd March, 1592/3 as excused from service as juror (B.M. Add. Ch. 5070, 5072)

Burials at Faccombe: Alice Willis, 29th July, 1646. Alice Willis, 23rd July, 1673 (2 burials for 3 Alices—? which).

John Willis m. Margerie Waterman at Linkenholt, 9th October, 1637. ? second marriage of John m. Rose Sherman. No issue found at Linkenholt.

A Luke Willis was buried at St. Maurice, Winchester, 2nd January, 1780. He may have been son of Luke of Ashmansworth (buried 1757) at Faccombe.

The burial of John Willis in 1742, assumed to be that of John (born 1678), might be that of John the pipe-maker (married 1718). There is a burial of a John Willis at Hamstead Marshall 18th December, 1715, which might be that of John (born 1678).

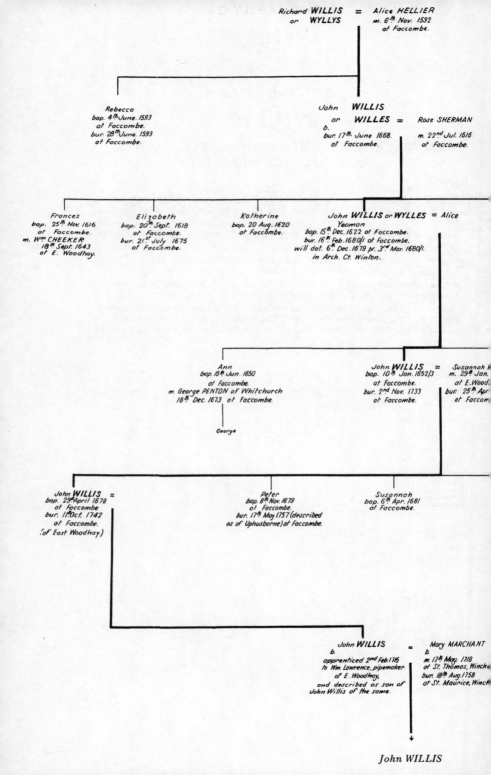

Richard **WILLIS** or **WYLLYS** = Alice **HELLIER**
m. 6ᵗʰ Nov. 1592 at Faccombe.

Rebecca
bap. 4ᵗʰ June. 1593
at Faccombe.
bur. 28ᵗʰ June. 1593
at Faccombe.

John **WILLIS** or **WILLES** = Rose **SHERMAN**
b.
bur. 17ᵗʰ June. 1668.
at Faccombe.
m. 22ⁿᵈ Jul. 1616
at Faccombe.

Frances
bap. 25ᵗʰ Nov. 1616
at Faccombe.
m. Wᵐ CHEEKER
18ᵗʰ Sept. 1643
of E. Woodhay.

Elizabeth
bap. 20ᵗʰ Sept. 1618
at Faccombe.
bur. 21ˢᵗ July 1675
at Faccombe.

Katherine
bap. 20 Aug. 1620
at Faccombe.

John **WILLIS** or **WYLLES** = Alice
Yeoman
bap. 15ᵗʰ Dec. 1622 at Faccombe.
bur. 16ᵗʰ Feb. 1680/1 at Faccombe.
will dat. 6ᵗʰ Dec. 1679 pr. 3ʳᵈ Mar. 1680/1.
in Arch. Ct. Winton.

Ann
bap. 15ᵗʰ Jun. 1650
at Faccombe.
m. George PENTON of Whitchurch
18ᵗʰ Dec. 1673 at Faccombe.

George

John **WILLIS** = Susannah
bap. 10ᵗʰ Jan. 1652/3   m. 29ᵗʰ Jan.
at Faccombe.   at E.Wood.
bur. 2ⁿᵈ Nov. 1733   bur. 25ᵗʰ Apr
at Faccombe.   at Faccomb

John **WILLIS** =
bap. 29ᵗʰ April 1678
at Faccombe.
bur. 11ᵗʰ Oct. 1742
at Faccombe.
(of East Woodhay.)

Peter
bap. 8ᵗʰ Nov. 1679
at Faccombe.
bur. 17ᵗʰ May 1757 (described
as of Uphusborne) at Faccombe.

Susannah
bap. 6ᵗʰ Apr. 1681
at Faccombe.

John **WILLIS**
b.
apprenticed 2ⁿᵈ Feb.1715
to Wm. Lawrence, pipemaker
of E.Woodhay,
and described as son of
John Willis of the same.

= Mary **MARCHANT**
b.
m. 17ᵗʰ May. 1718
at St. Thomas, Winch.
bur. 18ᵗʰ Aug. 1758
at St. Maurice, Winch.

John **WILLIS**

THE FAMILY OF
WILLIS
OF FACCOMBE AND WINCHESTER, HANTS., AND EALING, MIDDLESEX

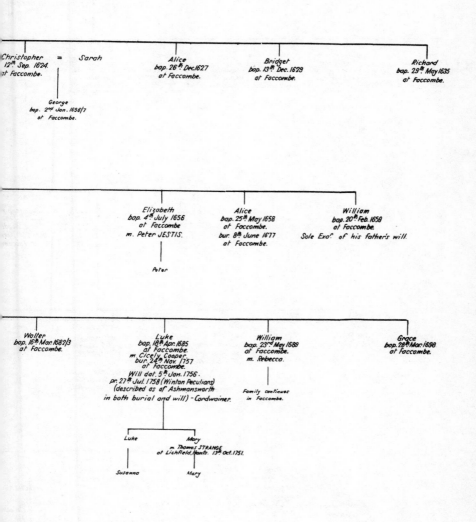

Christopher
12th Sep. 1624.
at Faccombe.
= Sarah

Alice
bap. 26th Dec.1627
at Faccombe.

Bridget
bap. 13th Dec. 1629
at Faccombe.

Richard
bap. 29th May 1635
at Faccombe.

George
bap. 2nd Jan. 1656/7
at Faccombe.

Elizabeth
bap. 4th July 1656
at Faccombe
m. Peter JESTIS.

Alice
bap. 25th May 1658
at Faccombe.
bur. 8th June 1677
at Faccombe.

William
bap. 20th Feb. 1659
at Faccombe.
Sole Exor. of his father's will.

Peter

Walter
bap. 16th Mar 1682/3
at Faccombe.

Luke
bap. 18th Apr. 1685
at Faccombe.
m. Cicely Cooper.
bur. 24th Nov. 1757
at Faccombe.
Will dat. 5th Jan. 1756.
pr. 27th Jul. 1758 (Wintan Peculiars)
(described as of Ashmansworth
in both burial and will) - Cordwainer.

William
bap. 23rd May 1689
at Faccombe.
m. Rebecca.

Family continues
in Faccombe.

Grace
bap. 28th Mar 1698
at Faccombe.

Luke

Mary
m. Thomas STRANGE
at Lichfield, Hants. 13th Oct. 1751.

Susanna

Mary

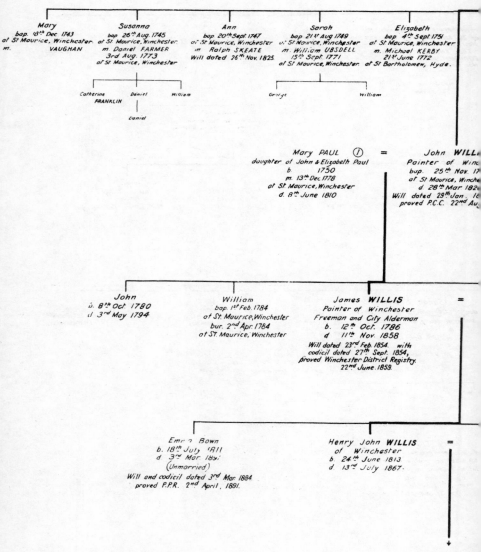

John WILL...

John WILLIS
of Middle Brooks, Winchester
b.
bur. 3rd Aug. 1783
at St. Maurice, Winchester

Mary
bap. 18th Dec 1743
at St Maurice, Winchester.
m.
VAUGHAN

Susanna
bap 26th Aug. 1745
at St. Maurice, Winchester
m Daniel FARMER
3rd Aug. 1773
at St Maurice, Winchester

Ann
bap. 20th Sept. 1747
at St Maurice, Winchester
m Ralph SKEATE
Will dated 26th Nov. 1825.

Sarah
bap 21st Aug 1749
at St Maurice, Winchester
m. William UBSDELL
15th Sept. 1771
at St Maurice, Winchester.

Elizabeth
bap 4th Sept. 1751
at St Maurice, Winchester
m. Michael KERBY
21st June 1772
of St Bartholomew, Hyde.

Catherine
FRANKLIN

Daniel

William

Daniel

George

William

Mary PAUL ① =
daughter of John & Elizabeth Paul
b.   1750
m. 13th Dec. 1778
at St. Maurice, Winchester
d. 8th June 1810

John WILL...
Painter of Winc...
bap. 25th Nov. 17...
at St. Maurice, Winche...
d. 28th Mar 182...
Will dated 29th Jan. 18...
proved P.C.C. 22nd Aug...

John
b. 8th Oct. 1780
d 3rd May 1794

William
bap. 1st Feb. 1784
at St. Maurice, Winchester
bur. 2nd Apr. 1784
at St. Maurice, Winchester

James WILLIS
Painter of Winchester
Freeman and City Alderman
b. 12th Oct. 1786
d 11th Nov. 1858
Will dated 23rd Feb. 1854. with
codicil dated 27th Sept. 1854,
proved Winchester District Registry.
22nd June 1859.

=

Emma Bown
b. 18th July 1811
d 3rd Mar. 1891
(Unmarried)
Will and codicil dated 3rd Mar 1884.
proved P.P.R. 2nd April, 1891.

Henry John WILLIS
of Winchester
b. 24th June 1813
d. 13rd July 1867.

=

James WILLIS

Mary RUMMEY

25ᵗʰ July. 1743
Maurice, Winchester.

Catherine	William	William	Laetitia Nicholson	Thomas
bap. 20ᵗʰ Apr. 1756 Maurice, Winchester. Thos. KNIGHT 20th Dec. 1795 Maurice, Winchester	bap. 29ᵗʰ May 1758 of St Maurice, Winchester bur. 25ᵗʰApl. 1759 of St Maurice, Winchester	bap 10ᵗʰ Aug. 1760 of St Maurice, Winchester bur. 11ᵗʰ Feb. 1763 of St. Maurice. Winchester.	bap 15ᵗʰ Apl. 1764. of St Maurice, Winchester m. William NAISH 15ᵗʰ May 1796 of St. Maurice, Winchester	bap. 13ᵗʰ Aug. 1766 of St Maurice, Winchester. bur. 14ᵗʰ Feb. 1768 of St. Maurice, Winchester.

William   John NAISH   Harriet   Elizabeth   Anne
Schoolmaster, Trafalgar House School
Mayor of Winchester 1858-59.

② Mary WHITE
b. 1764
m.
d. 2ⁿᵈ Nov 1846

Will dated 20ᵗʰ Aug. 1838. and codicils
proved P.C.C. 17ᵗʰ Mar. 1847.

Walter   Nellie   Godfrey   Sidney
Rector of Littleton   of Alton
m. Hayles.

Sarah BOWN	Ann	Mary
dau. of Benjamin & Hannah Bown sister of Mary, wife of Richard Gover b m. 9ᵗʰ Oct. 1810, by licence. at St. Cross. Winchester d. 27ᵗʰ Mar 1850	b. 1788 or 1789 m. John Ralph SKEATE of Sarum (step son of her Aunt Ann) 18ᵗʰ May 1809 at St Mary Kalendar, Winchester d. 20ᵗʰ Apl. 1831.	bap. 3ʳᵈ July 1791 of St. Maurice, Winchester bur. 7ᵗʰ July 1791 of St. Maurice, Winchester

Willis   George   John Henry   Thomas   Sarah Ann   ?

Mary TRIMBEE	Maria
of William Trimbee (in 1868 89 & senior brother of the tal of St. Cross, Winchester) b. 12ᵗʰ Jan. 1810 m. 11ᵗʰ June 1837 at St. James's, Westminster. d. 23ʳᵈ Jan. 1889	b. 13ᵗʰ Aug. 1815 d. 27ᵗʰ June 1876 (Unmarried). Will dated 15ᵗʰ Sep. 1865. pr. at Winchester 5ᵗʰ July, 1876.

Sarah Elizabeth

b. 28th June 1837
m. Richard SNOW
Miller, of Abbotsworthy, Winchester.
25th Jan. 1865
at St. Peter, Cheesehill, Winchester.

James Herbert **WILLIS** L.R.I.B.A.
Architect, H.M. Office of Works
of Ealing, Middlesex and the
British Embassy, Constantinople
b. 4th March 1864
d. 15th Dec. 1950
Will dated 17th Nov. 1944 and
codicil dated 14th Mar. 1947,
proved P.P.R. 24th Jan. 1951.

=

Annie Elizabeth PAPAZOGLU
dau. of George & Sarah Papazoglu
b. 13th Aug. 1871
m. 29th Jan 1894
at British Consulate-General and
Constantinople.
d. 24th Mar. 1939

Arthur James **WILLIS** F.R.C.S.
Chartered Quantity Surveyor
of Ealing, Middlesex &
Lyminge, Kent.
b. 16th Jan 1895
at Constantinople
d. 26 Nov 1983

=

Audrey Isabel Edith THOMPSON
dau. of Thomas Moore-Lane and
Isabel Mary THOMPSON of Ealing
b. 5th July 1897
m. at St. John's Ealing
3rd. Aug 1918
d. 29 Sep 1981

Cicely Mary
B.A. (Lond.)
b. 29th Nov. 1922
m. at Lyminge, Kent.
17th June 1950

=

John Norman CAPENER
M.A. (Cantab), M.I.C.E.
son of Norman Capener, F.R.C.S.
of Exeter, Devon.
b. 23rd Aug. 1924.

Christopher James **WILLIS** F.R.I.C.S.
b. 25th May 1928
at Ealing, Middlesex.

=

James Andrew WILLIS
B.Sc., A.R.I.C.S.
b. 2 Oct 1957

=

Moira Patricia
dau of Dermot
James and
Eileen RUSSELL
b. 28 May 1957
m. 15 Oct 1983

Jane Rosemary
b. 28 Jan 1959
d. 28 Jan 1960

Henry John WILLIS

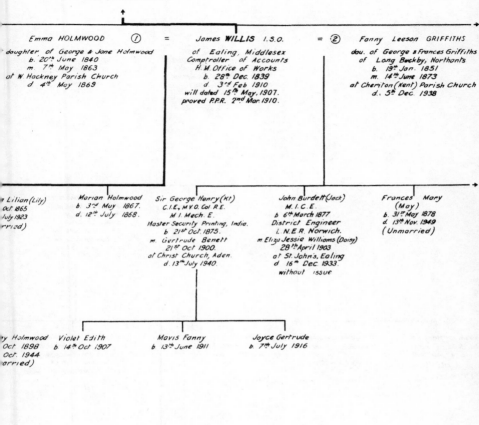

Emma HOLMWOOD ① =	James **WILLIS** I.S.O. = ②	Fanny Leeson GRIFFITHS
daughter of George & Jane Holmwood	of Ealing, Middlesex	dau. of George & Frances Griffiths
b. 20ᵗʰ June 1840	Comptroller of Accounts	of Long Buckby, Northants
m. 7ᵗʰ May 1863	H.M. Office of Works	b. 19ᵗʰ Jan. 1851
at W. Hackney Parish Church	b. 28ᵗʰ Dec. 1839	m. 14ᵗʰ June 1873
d 4ᵗʰ May 1869	d. 3ʳᵈ Feb 1910	at Cheriton (Kent) Parish Church
	will dated 15ᵗʰ May, 1907.	d. 5ᵗʰ Dec. 1938
	proved P.P.R. 2ⁿᵈ Mar. 1910.	

m Lilian (Lily)
Oct 1865
July 1923
(arried)

Marian Holmwood
b. 3ʳᵈ May 1867.
d. 12ᵗʰ July 1868.

Sir George Henry (Kt)
C.I.E., M.V.O. Col. R.E.
M.I. Mech. E.
Master Security Printing, India.
b 21ˢᵗ Oct. 1875.
m. Gertrude Benett
21ˢᵗ Oct 1900.
at Christ Church, Aden.
d. 13ᵗʰ July 1940.

John Burdett (Jack)
M.I.C.E.
b 6ᵗʰ March 1877
District Engineer
L.N.E.R. Norwich.
m Eliza Jessie Williams (Daisy)
28ᵗʰ April 1903
at St. John's, Ealing
d 16ᵗʰ Dec. 1933.
without issue

Frances Mary
(May)
b. 31ˢᵗ May 1878
d. 13ᵗʰ Nov. 1949
(Unmarried)

y Holmwood
Oct 1898
Oct. 1944
(arried)

Violet Edith
b 14ᵗʰ Oct 1907

Mavis Fanny
b 13ᵗʰ June 1911

Joyce Gertrude
b. 7ᵗʰ July 1916

hy Elaine WILLIS
11ᵗʰ Oct. 1921
Malmesbury, Wilts.
24ᵗʰ April 1954
Purton, Wilts.

n Simon =
Oct 1961

Christine Irene
dau of James and
Kathleen WATTS
of Caterham,
Surrey
b. 30 Jan 1962
m. 30 July 1983

Philip Brian
b. 29 Nov 1963

Emma

b. 5ᵗʰ Nov. 1841
m. Thomas Alfred JONES
Jeweller, of Islington.
at St. Paul's, Islington
5ᵗʰ May 1863

Frank Reginald
C.B.E., Capt. R.N
Chief Inspector of Naval
Ordnance, Admiralty
b. 9ᵗʰ Aug. 1881
m. Pauline Mann (Poppy)
14ᵗʰ May 1908
at St. John's, Ealing.
d. 8ᵗʰ April 1964.

Richard
M.A. (Oxon.)
b. 24ᵗʰ June 1887
Temp Lieut Loyal N. Lancs.
Regt. Killed in Action
16ᵗʰ May 1916
(Unmarried)

Norman Steward
M.A. (Oxon;) Vicar of
Purton, Wilts. & Hon.
Canon of Bristol
b. 29ᵗʰ Oct. 1894.
m. Eileen Mary Burke
at St. John's, Ealing.
1ˢᵗ March 1919.

Frances Mary (Molly)
B.Sc. (Lond.)
b. 24ᵗʰ Mar. 1909
d. 2 Jul 1980
(unmarried)

Eugenie Leeson
M.A., M.B., B.Ch. (Cantab)
F.R.C.S., L.R.C.P.
b. 23ʳᵈ July 1910.
d. 12ᵗʰ Sept. 1948.
(Unmarried)

Pamela Leslie
B.A. (Cantab)
b. 28ᵗʰ Mar. 1914

Angela Christine
M.B., B.Ch.
b. 23ʳᵈ June 1929
m. Denis FOWLER
M.B., B.Ch.

INDEX

Titles of books are given in italics and are arranged according to subject. Reference should also be made to the bibliography on pages 102 to 108, as these books are not included unless mentioned in the text.

Indexing of the second part of the book is limited to instances in the story illustrating the practical application of matters mentioned in the first part.

TABLE OF STATUTES